BASE

BASIC ADULT SURVIVAL ENGLISH

with orientation to american life

ROBERT E. WALSH

Basic
Adult
Survival
English

*with orientation
to american life*

PART ONE

ROBERT E. WALSH

Prentice-Hall, Inc., Englewood Cliffs, New Jersey 07632

Library of Congress Cataloging in Publication Data

Walsh, Robert E. (date)
 Basic adult survival English.

 1. English language—Text-books for foreign speakers.
2. Americanisms. I. Title. II. Title: American life.
PE1128.W34 1984   428.2′4   83–19046
ISBN 0–13–056812–0 (v. 1)
ISBN 0–13–056854–6 (v. 2)

Editorial/production supervision and
  interior design: Elizabeth H. Athorn
Cover design: Ben Santora
Manufacturing buyer: Harry P. Baisley
Interior art: Virgilio Salvador and Don Martinetti
Page layout: Meg Van Arsdale

Printed in the United States of America

10 9 8 7 6 5 4 3

ISBN 0-13-056812-0

Prentice-Hall International, Inc., *London*
Prentice-Hall of Australia Pty. Limited, *Sydney*
Editora Prentice-Hall do Brasil, Ltda., *Rio de Janeiro*
Prentice-Hall Canada Inc., *Toronto*
Prentice-Hall of India Private Limited, *New Delhi*
Prentice-Hall of Japan, Inc., *Tokyo*
Prentice-Hall of Southeast Asia Pte. Ltd., *Singapore*
Whitehall Books Limited, *Wellington, New Zealand*

Contents

3. HOUSING:

4. DIRECTIONS AND TRANSPORTATION:

5. HEALTH CARE:

Preface

Basic Adult Survival English (BASE) is a high-beginning to intermediate level survival ESL textbook in two volumes. It is designed to provide adult learners with basic language proficiency, survival skills, and information about life in the United States. It is particularly aimed at helping newcomers to the United States to become functioning members of American society.

BASE can serve as a core text, providing a foundation for the study of basic ESL, or it may be used as a convenient and effective supplement to existing texts. BASE may be used "cover to cover": Chapters develop in complexity of content and grammar, with continual built-in review of preceding material. It is also possible to pull out individual chapters, such as the Health Care chapter from *Part One* or the Driving chapter from *Part Two*, and use them independently.

The two volumes of BASE are each divided into five chapters that deal with essential survival areas. Each chapter topic is treated thoroughly, with continuity from first page to last. Key features of BASE are as follows:

• Situational conversations present natural language in relevant settings.
• New vocabulary is presented primarily through pictures.
• Structure sections present grammar points and provide practice through examples, writing exercises, and paired student activities.
• Orientation sections explain aspects of American life and offer ideas on coping with a new social and cultural environment. The language used reinforces content and structures presented in the particular chapter. Topics include, for example, "The American Family" and "Taking Care of Your House" in *Part One* or "Buying on Credit" and "Finding a Job" in *Part Two*. Orientation sections may also be used for reading practice.
• Action Sequences engage the student in the ordered physical performance of activities, such as "Taking the Bus" and "Spraying for Insects" in *Part One* or "Buying Coffee from a Vending Machine" in *Part Two*.
• Self-Tests enable students to evaluate their progress as they proceed through the text.

• Listening and Speaking pages at the end of each chapter offer students practice in discriminating and producing English sounds occurring in the chapter.

Each chapter is prefaced by a statement of its curriculum objectives: competencies, orientation topics, and structures. Teacher notes at the beginning of each chapter offer suggestions for use and additional classroom activities.

Introductory Notes and Suggestions for Teachers

Teacher Notes and Suggestions sections at the beginning of each chapter of BASE give page-by-page recommendations of approaches and particular points of emphasis. Here are some general suggestions for use of the text.

1. Before referring to any printed page, the class should first practice orally the language involved. The teacher may want to present and practice beforehand structures and vocabulary to be introduced, or may want to have them learned in context. When a page is set in a particular context, that context should be explained to the students to aid in the transition from oral to written language.

2. Conversations or dialogues may be effectively presented as described below. After setting the situation of the dialogue, and perhaps explaining new vocabulary, the teacher introduces the dialogue orally following these steps:

   • Teacher models dialogue, students listen.
   • Teacher models dialogue, students repeat.
   • Class performs dialogue, half of class taking one side, half the other, repeating after the teacher.
   • Class performs dialogue again on teacher's visual cue.
   • Teacher takes one side of dialogue, class other.
   • Student-student pairs model dialogue for class.
   • Class divides into pairs and practices dialogue; teacher listens.

   The written dialogue may be referred to for reinforcement at any point that the teacher sees it is necessary.

3. Vocabulary on vocabulary pages should be presented with realia when possible. Words may be practiced using a great variety of techniques, including visuals, picture cards, dyads, memory games, association exercises, and so on.

4. Orientation Notes: The teacher first sets the context, relating the topic to the particular lesson. The teacher introduces the point in his/her own words and whenever possible relates the topic to the students' experience and native customs. The teacher then reads the passage in sections and explains it, asking comprehension questions. Then the teacher reads the page line by line and has the students repeat. The teacher should foster class discussion. Passages may later be used for reading practice.

5. Action Sequences: An effective procedure for presenting and practicing Action Sequences is as follows:

   • Teacher says and acts out each step; students watch and listen. (The teacher may wish to pantomime the entire sequence first.)
   • Teacher says and acts out each step; class repeats.
   • Teacher acts out each line and class says each line.
   • Individual students perform the sequence in front of the class saying each line.
   • Individual students perform the sequence in front of the class as seated students in turn give them commands.

   The printed page should be referred to at the appropriate point for reinforcement.

6. Self-Tests can be administered as the teacher desires. Dictations and other tests can be made up by drawing from the text.

7. Listening and Speaking exercises at the end of each chapter cover all the common consonant sounds in initial and final positions and all the common vowel sounds and diphthongs. All words on any one page are drawn from the chapter involved. Additional sound contrasts can be practiced by referring to Listening and Speaking pages previously studied. Pronunciation difficulties will vary for students of different language groups; the teacher should give problem sounds special emphasis. Words in Part C have been syllabicated on the basis of pronunciation.

THE ENGLISH ALPHABET

a b c d e f g h i j k l m n o p q r s t u v w x y z

A B C D E F G H I J K L M N O P Q R S T U V W X Y Z

a b c d e f g h i j k l m n o p q r s t u v w x y z

A B C D E F G H I J K L M N O P Q R S T U V W X Y Z

NUMBERS

1	one	11	eleven	30	thirty	1st	first
2	two	12	twelve	40	forty	2nd	second
3	three	13	thirteen	50	fifty	3rd	third
4	four	14	fourteen	60	sixty	4th	fourth
5	five	15	fifteen	70	seventy	5th	fifth
6	six	16	sixteen	80	eighty	6th	sixth
7	seven	17	seventeen	90	ninety	7th	seventh
8	eight	18	eighteen	100	one hundred	8th	eighth
9	nine	19	nineteen	200	two hundred	9th	ninth
10	ten	20	twenty	1,000	one thousand	10th	tenth
		21	twenty-one	10,000	ten thousand		
		22	twenty-two	100,000	one hundred thousand		
				1,000,000	one million		

DAYS
Monday
Tuesday
Wednesday
Thursday
Friday
Saturday
Sunday

MONTHS
January	July
February	August
March	September
April	October
May	November
June	December

Personal Information

chapter one

COMPETENCIES:	1. Give and ask for information about oneself and one's family
	2. Fill out simple information forms
	3. Get data from identification papers
	4. Make introductions appropriately
ORIENTATION:	1. American use of names and titles
	2. Use and importance of identification
STRUCTURES:	1. Subject pronouns
	2. Present tense *be*: affirmative, negative, interrogative, contractions, short answers
	3. *Wh*-questions
	4. Possessive adjectives
	5. Possessive form of nouns

Teacher Notes and Suggestions

Page 3
1. First present your own name and the names of several students, pointing out American use of names: (a) the order is first name then last name; (b) friends are addressed by their first names; (c) the last name is used with a title (Mr., Mrs., Miss, etc.) to show respect.
2. The address is read "forty-two fifty-seven"; other numbers here are read digit by digit.
3. Explain the use of *my* and *your.*

Page 4
1. Point out the use of subject pronouns *I, you.*
2. Point out the contraction *I am, I'm.*
3. Point out that *you* is used to address everyone (old, young, male, female, formal, familiar) and that it is used for both singular and plural.
4. "How old are you?" and sometimes "Are you married?" are considered personal questions by Americans and are not commonly asked.

Page 5
Demonstrate first with people in class, introducing first the pronouns, then the corresponding verb, then the contracted forms.

Page 7
1. Point out alternate contracted forms in Part D.
2. Point out inversion of subject and verb in question form (Part E).

Page 8
Point out that a contraction alone cannot be used as a short answer.

Pages 9 to 10
1. Have a student come to the front of the class and introduce him- or herself by giving information as in the examples. Ask questions of the class about the student. After working with several students in this way, male and female, put the face and information from Part A on the board, practice the statements, and then ask the questions. Have students then complete Parts A, B, and C.
2. Point out the difference between country of origin and nationality (e.g., Italy/Italian).

Page 11
1. Teach the meaning of the terms involved or have students learn them as sight words.
2. Point out that the last name appears first on many forms.
3. Point out that the date is written month/day/year.

Page 12
Explain the various types of identification.

Page 13
Have students fill in information on all cards, copying from their own identification papers. If they don't have an item, they should fill it out anyway.

Page 14
1. Present and practice the dialogue in Part A orally first, using students in the class, with variations for man and woman.
2. Explain how to make introductions and how to be introduced, including handshake, etc. Mention that Americans expect to be introduced to people they don't know.

Page 15
Point out the meaning of the possessive construction *daughter's friend.*

Page 16
Explain the formation and use of the possessive form of nouns and the positions of the form before the noun modified.

Page 18
Students should write information about their own family members, adjusting the exercise as appropriate.

What's Your Name?

Read and practice.

Hello!
My name is Dan Lee.
My first name is Dan.
My last name is Lee.
My address is 4257 Spring Street.
My zip code is 92115.
My telephone number is 582–3607.

Write about yourself.

My name is _____.

My first name is _____.

My last name is _____.

My address is _____.

My zip code is _____.

My telephone number is _____.

Now practice with another student.

Hi!
What's your name?
What's your first name?
What's your last name?
What's your address?
What's your zip code?
What's your telephone number?

Where Are You From?

Read and practice.

My name is Dan Lee.
I am from Vietnam.
I'm Vietnamese.
I am 35.
I'm married.
I have two children.

Answer the questions about yourself and practice with another student.

1. What's your name? _____

2. Where are you from? _____

3. Are you American? _____

4. How old are you? _____

5. Are you married? _____

6. Do you have any children? _____

structure practice

Study.

I am a student.
I'm a student.

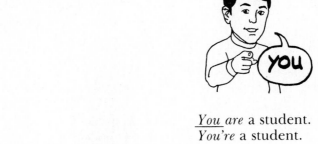

You are a student.
You're a student.

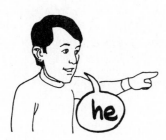

He is a student.
He's a student.

We are students.
We're students.

She is a student.
She's a student.

They are students.
They're students.

It is a pencil.
It's a pencil.

structure practice

A *Study. Then fill in the blanks.*

<table>
<tr><td>I</td><td>he</td><td>she</td><td>they</td></tr>
<tr><td>I <u>am</u> from Vietnam.</td><td>He <u>is</u> from New York.</td><td>She <u>is</u> from Mexico.</td><td>They <u>are</u> from France.</td></tr>
<tr><td>I <u>am</u> Vietnamese.</td><td>He <u>is</u> American.</td><td>She __ Mexican.</td><td>They ____ French.</td></tr>
<tr><td>I ___ married.</td><td>He __ married.</td><td>She __ single.</td><td>They ____ married.</td></tr>
<tr><td>I ___ 35.</td><td>He __ 28.</td><td>She __ 19.</td><td></td></tr>
</table>

B *Study these contractions.*

I am ⟶ (I ám) ⟶ I'm

he is ⟶ (he ís) ⟶ he's
she is ⟶ (she ís) ⟶ she's
it is ⟶ (it ís) ⟶ it's

you are ⟶ (you áre) ⟶ you're
we are ⟶ (we áre) ⟶ we're
they are ⟶ (they áre) ⟶ they're

Now change the sentences in Part A to contractions.

<table>
<tr><td><u>I'm</u> from Vietnam.</td><td><u>He's</u> from New York.</td><td><u>She's</u> from Mexico.</td><td><u>They're</u> from France.</td></tr>
<tr><td>____ Vietnamese.</td><td>____ American.</td><td>____ Mexican.</td><td>_____ French.</td></tr>
<tr><td>____ married.</td><td>____ married.</td><td>____ single.</td><td>_____ married.</td></tr>
<tr><td>____ 35.</td><td>____ 28.</td><td>____ 19.</td><td></td></tr>
</table>

C *Study these examples.*

Affirmative	Negative
You are married.	You are *not* married.
He is a student.	He is *not* a student.
Dan is a student.	Dan is *not* a student.
They are American.	They are *not* American.

Write the negative.

1. She is American.   <u>She is not American.</u>

2. He is Mexican.   _____

3. I am from Vietnam.   _____

4. You are a refugee.   _____

5. English is easy.   _____

6. They are my children.   _____

D *Study these contractions.*

I am not	→ I'm not		
he is not	→ he's not	-or-	he isn't
she is not	→ she's not	-or-	she isn't
it is not	→ it's not	-or-	it isn't
you are not	→ you're not	-or-	you aren't
we are not	→ we're not	-or-	we aren't
they are not	→ they're not	-or-	they aren't

Now change the negatives in Part C to contractions.

1. She's not American.   She isn't American.

2. _____   _____

3. _____   _____

4. _____   _____

5. _____   _____

6. _____   _____

E *Study these examples.*

Affirmative	Questions
You are married.	*Are you* married?
He is a student.	*Is he* a student?
Dan is a student.	*Is Dan* a student?
They are American.	*Are they* American?

Write the questions.

1. You are married.   Are you married?

2. She is a student.   _____

3. He is Vietnamese.   _____

4. Dan is married.   _____

5. English is hard.   _____

Now look at the answers and write the questions.

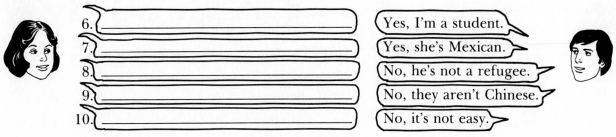

6. _____   Yes, I'm a student.

7. _____   Yes, she's Mexican.

8. _____   No, he's not a refugee.

9. _____   No, they aren't Chinese.

10. _____   No, it's not easy.

F *Study these examples. Then practice with another student.*

Questions	Answers	Short answers
1. Are you married?	-Yes, I'm married. -No, I'm not married.	-Yes, I am. -No, I'm not.
2. Is he a student? (Is Dan a student?)	-Yes, he's a student. -No, he's not a student. -No, he isn't a student.	-Yes, he is. -No, he is not. -No, he's isn't.
3. Are they American?	-Yes, they're American. -No, they're not American. -No, they aren't American.	-Yes, they are. -No, they're not. -No, they aren't.

Write the short answer.

1. Are you a student? Yes, _____
2. Are you married? No, _____
3. Is your teacher American? Yes, _____
4. Is English easy? No, _____
5. Are your children at school? Yes, _____

structure practice

Study. Then fill in the blanks.

__my__ name
__my__ address
__my__ telephone number

__your__ name
__your__ address
_____ telephone number

__his__ name
_____ address
_____ telephone number

__her__ name
_____ address
_____ telephone number

__our__ house
_____ children
_____ car

__their__ house
_____ children
_____ car

What's His Name? What's Her Name?

Look at the pictures and answer the questions. Then practice with another student.

A

My name is Jerry Morton.　　　I'm 28.
My first name is Jerry.　　　I'm married.
My last name is Morton.　　　I'm American.
My address is 2240 Dale Street.　　I'm from New York.

1. What's his name? _____

2. What's his first name? _____

3. What's his last name? _____

4. What's his address? _____

5. How old is he? _____

6. Is he married? _____

7. Is he American? _____

8. Where is he from? _____

B

My name is Ana Lopez.
My first name is Ana.
My last name is Lopez.
　　I'm a student.
　　I'm from Mexico.
　　I'm Mexican.
　　I'm not married.

Write the answers.

1. What's her name? _____

2. What's her first name? _____

3. What's her last name? _____

4. Where is she from? _____

5. Is she a student? _____

6. Is she married? _____

C

My name is Tony Parelli.
My address is 4317 35th Street.
My telephone number is 365-0998.
I'm from Italy.
I'm Italian.
I'm 33.

Write the questions.

1. What's _____ name?   His name is Tony Parelli.

2. What's _____ _____?   His address is 4317 35th St.

3. _____ _____ _____ _____?   His telephone number is 365-0998.

4. Where ____ ____ _____?   He's from Italy.

5. ____ ____ _____?   Yes, he's Italian.

6. _____ _____ ____ ____?   He's 33.

Filling Out Forms

Study.

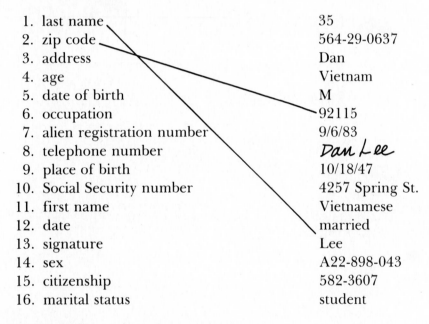

INFORMATION FORM

Name (Mr.) Mrs. Miss: *Lee* (last) *Dan* (first) *35* (age) *M* (sex)

Address *4257* (number) *Spring Street* (street) *582-3607* (telephone)

San Diego (city) *CA* (state) *92115* (zip code) *married* (marital status)

Social Security No. *564-29-0637*   Alien Reg. No. *A22-898-043*

10/18/47 (date of birth)   *Vietnam* (place of birth)   *Vietnamese* (citizenship)

Occupation *student*   *9/6/83* (date)   *Dan Lee* (signature)

Draw a line and match the words.

1. last name
2. zip code
3. address
4. age
5. date of birth
6. occupation
7. alien registration number
8. telephone number
9. place of birth
10. Social Security number
11. first name
12. date
13. signature
14. sex
15. citizenship
16. marital status

35
564-29-0637
Dan
Vietnam
M
92115
9/6/83
Dan Lee
10/18/47
4257 Spring St.
Vietnamese
married
Lee
A22-898-043
582-3607
student

Now fill out this form for yourself.

INFORMATION FORM

Name: Mr. Mrs. Miss ___ (last) ___ (first) ___ (age) ___ (sex)

Address ___ (number) ___ (street) ___ (telephone)

___ (city) ___ (state) ___ (zip code) ___ (marital status)

Social Security No. ___   Alien Reg. No. ___

___ (date of birth)   ___ (place of birth)   ___ (citizenship)

Occupation ___   ___ (date)   ___ (signature)

Identification

Study.

Social Security Card

Identification Card (ID card)

Driver's License

Permanent Resident
Alien Card (Green Card)

WARNING
• A NONIMMIGRANT WHO ACCEPTS UNAUTHORIZED EMPLOYMENT IS SUBJECT TO DEPORTATION.
  IMPORTANT
• RETAIN THIS PERMIT IN YOUR POSSESSION: YOU MUST SURRENDER IT WHEN YOU LEAVE THE U.S. FAILURE TO DO SO MAY DELAY YOUR ENTRY INTO THE U.S. IN THE FUTURE.

ADMISSION NUMBER
995-01625908

ADMITTED AS A REFUGEE PURSUANT TO SEC. 207 OF THE I & N ACT
EMPLOYMENT AUTHORIZED

SEA JUL 27 1983 195

IF YOU DEPART THE U.S. YOU WILL NEED PRIOR PERMISSION FROM INS TO RETURN.

FAMILY NAME (SURNAME)
L E E
FIRST (GIVEN) NAME
D A N

DATE OF BIRTH
DAY | MO. | YR.
1 8 | 0 3 | 6 4

COUNTRY OF CITIZENSHIP
V I E T N A M
SEE REVERSE SIDE FOR OTHER IMPORTANT INFORMATION

U.S. IMMIGRATION AND NATURALIZATION SERVICE

1-94 DEPARTURE RECORD
(REV. 1-1-83)

STAPLE HERE

Alien Registration Card (Form I-94)

Answer these questions.

1. What is Dan Lee's address? _____

2. Where is he from? _____

3. What is his Social Security number? _____

4. What is his alien registration number? _____

5. What is his birth date? _____

Now write your information.

Show me your identification.

SOCIAL SECURITY

- - -
NUMBER

NAME

SIGNATURE

Social Security Card

IDENTIFICATION CARD
NOT A LICENSE / FOR IDENTIFICATION ONLY

NAME _____

ADDRESS _____

CITY _____ STATE _____ ZIP _____

SEX _____

BIRTHDATE _____

SIGNATURE

Identification Card

DRIVER LICENSE

NUMBER _____

NAME _____

ADDRESS _____

CITY _____ STATE _____ ZIP _____

SEX _____

BIRTHDATE _____

SIGNATURE

Driver's License

RESIDENT ALIEN

NAME _____ / _____
LAST   FIRST

DATE OF BIRTH

ALIEN NUMBER

SIGNATURE

Permanent Resident
Alien Card (Green Card)

WARNING
- A NONIMMIGRANT WHO ACCEPTS UNAUTHORIZED EMPLOYMENT IS SUBJECT TO DEPORTATION.
  IMPORTANT
- RETAIN THIS PERMIT IN YOUR POSSESSION: YOU MUST SURRENDER IT WHEN YOU LEAVE THE U.S. FAILURE TO DO SO MAY DELAY YOUR ENTRY INTO THE U.S. IN THE FUTURE.

ADMISSION NUMBER
995-01625908

ADMITTED AS A REFUGEE PURSUANT TO SEC. 207 OF THE I & N ACT
EMPLOYMENT AUTHORIZED

SEA JUL 27 1983 195

IF YOU DEPART THE U.S. YOU WILL NEED PRIOR PERMISSION FROM INS TO RETURN.

FAMILY NAME (SURNAME)

FIRST (GIVEN) NAME

DATE OF BIRTH | COUNTRY OF CITIZENSHIP

DAY | MO. | YR.

SEE REVERSE SIDE FOR OTHER IMPORTANT INFORMATION

U.S. IMMIGRATION AND NATURALIZATION SERVICE | 1-94 DEPARTURE RECORD (REV. 1-1-83) | STAPLE HERE

Alien Registration Card (Form I-94)

Introductions

A *Study. Then complete the conversations.*

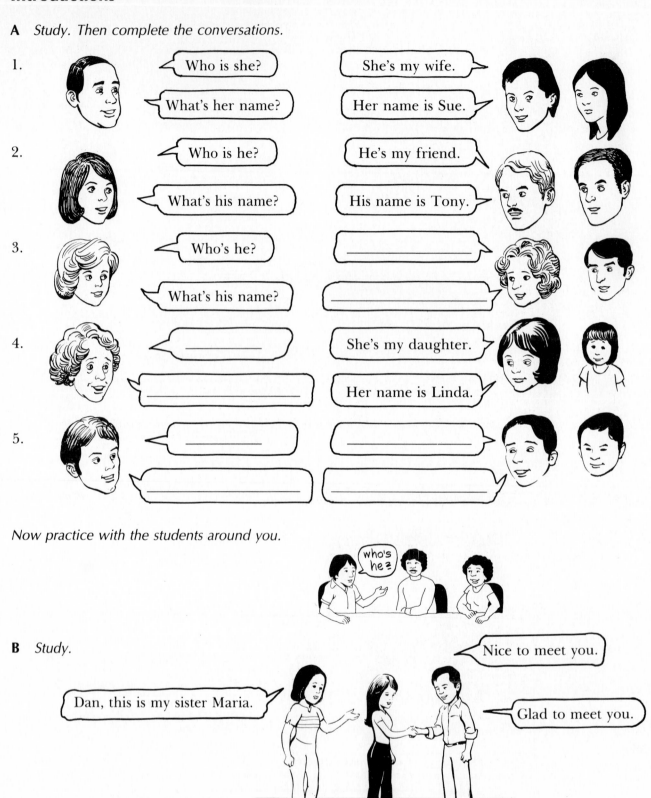

1. Who is she? — She's my wife.
   What's her name? — Her name is Sue.

2. Who is he? — He's my friend.
   What's his name? — His name is Tony.

3. Who's he? — _____
   What's his name? — _____

4. _____ — She's my daughter.
   _____ — Her name is Linda.

5. _____ — _____
   _____ — _____

Now practice with the students around you.

who's he?

B *Study.*

Dan, this is my sister Maria.

Nice to meet you.

Glad to meet you.

Now practice making introductions with other students.

structure practice

A *Write the questions and answers. Then practice with another student.*

my brother
Sam
25
in my country
fine

1. Who __is he_____ ? ____He's my brother._____
2. What's _his name_____ ? _____
3. How old _____? ? _____
4. Where _____? ? _____
5. How _____? ? _____

B *Write the questions and answers. Then practice with another student.*

my daughter's friend
Sally
about 15
in California
fine

1. ___Who_____? ? _____
2. _____? ? _____
3. _____? ? _____
4. _____? ? _____
5. _____? ? _____

structure practice

A *Study. Then fill in the blanks.*

Dan

Dan<u>'s</u> wife   Dan<u>'s</u> daughter   Dan__ son

_____ house

_____ family

B *Fill in the blanks.*

1. my wife	<u>my wife's</u>	name	<u>my wife's</u>	family
2. my husband	<u>my husband's</u>	name	_____	mother
3. your brother	_____	name	_____	friend
4. her daughter	_____	name	_____	school
5. their son	_____	name	_____	teacher
6. my friend	_____	name	_____	house

Dan's Family

Study.

Dan
35
husband

Sue
29
wife

Mae
6
daughter

Timmy
2
son

Practice this conversation.

Are you married?

Yes, I am.

Do you have any children?

Yes, I have two.

How many boys and how many girls?

One boy and one girl.

Fill in the conversations.

1.   What's your wife's name?

    How old is she?

    Her name is Sue.

    She's 29.

2.   What's your husband's name?

    How old is he?

    _____ Dan.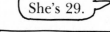

    _____ 35.

3.   What's your daughter's name?

    How old _____

    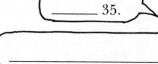

4. _____

    _____

Your Family

A *Fill in the blanks. Then answer the questions about your family and practice with another student.*

| father | mother | sister | brother |

name _____ _____ _____ _____

age _____ _____ _____ _____

   1. What's your father's name? _____

   2. How old is he? _____

   3. What's your mother's name? _____

   4. How old is she? _____

   5. How many brothers and sisters do you have? _____

   6. What's your sister's name? _____

   7. How old is she? _____

   8. What's your brother's name? _____

   9. How old is he? _____

B | husband | wife | daughter | son |

name _____ _____ _____ _____

age _____ _____ _____ _____

   1. Are you married? _____

   2. What's your husband's name? _____

   3. How old is he? _____

   4. What's your wife's name? _____

   5. How old is she? _____

   6. Do you have any children? _____

   7. How many do you have? _____

   8. How many boys and how many girls? _____

   9. What are their names? _____

  10. How old are they? _____

listening and speaking

A *Listen to your teacher pronounce these words. Then listen again and repeat. Then listen to your teacher pronounce the key words below, and write under them the words that have the same sound in the same position. Check the word after you use it (√); use some words twice (√) (√).*

his (√)   name ( ) ( )   form ( ) ( )
nice ( )   father ( )   write ( ) ( )
date ( ) ( )   have ( )

1	2	3	4	5	6
how	first	meet	am	age	wife
his					

B *Circle the cluster and pronounce.*

(fr)om   friend   brother   student   state   (str)eet   Spring

C *Your teacher will pronounce these words. Listen and repeat.*

fa mi ly   A me ri can   Ca li for nia   i den ti fi ca tion
te le phone

Food and Shopping

chapter two

COMPETENCIES:
1. Tell time
2. Ask for and give location of stored items
3. Shop in a supermarket
4. Order in a fast food restaurant

ORIENTATION:
1. Scheduling of daily activities
2. American food
3. Supermarkets and shopping procedures
4. Fast food restaurants

STRUCTURES:
1. Introduction of present tense of *do* verbs
2. Prepositions of position
3. Adverbs of frequency
4. Noun plurals

Teacher Notes and Suggestions

Page 22   Act out the Action Sequences first (follow the procedure recommended on page *ix*).

Page 24   Use this as a basis for teaching telling time.

Page 25   Mention that most people have a daily routine, a schedule that they follow.

Page 26   Vocabulary may be practiced as suggested on page *ix*.

Page 27   Present prepositions of position introduced at the top of the page by demonstration. Then practice in the classroom using real objects. Then introduce the picture and exercises. Point out the pronoun substitution in the answer *(it/they)* and the corresponding verb forms *(is/are)*.

Page 31   Ask if any students are familiar with American food and what students usually eat at meals.

Page 32   After practicing the Action Sequence, take an imaginary plate of chicken around the class, asking "How does it look? How does it smell? How does it taste?"

Page 33   1. Precede with a discussion of stores and food shopping in the students' native countries.
    2. Demonstrate and practice the Action Sequence as recommended.

Page 34   After presenting and practicing the dialogue, have the students list other items on the board. Working in pairs, they will ask the location of each item and provide the answer by consulting the aisle signs.

Page 35   Explain usages of various adverbs of frequency by means of the percent scale.

Page 36   Point out that numbers 1–8, numbers 9–16 and numbers 17–24 correspond to pronunciations /-z/, /-s/, and /-iz/, respectively.

Page 37   The various containers should be introduced with realia, if possible, and practiced in such situations as *"Get me a jar of coffee."*

Page 39   1. Take students on a visit to a fast food restaurant, if possible, with assignments of things to look for, such as prices, signs, location of napkins, and so on. Good nutrition may also be brought up here.
    2. In working on conversation *1*, have students add the total of the food ($1.70). Explain that most states charge sales tax (in this example, 11¢).

■ *action sequence* ➡

every morning

1. I get up.
2. I go to the bathroom.
3. I wash my face.
4. I brush my teeth.
5. I comb my hair.
6. I put on my clothes.
7. I go to the kitchen.
8. I eat breakfast.
9. I wash the dishes.
10. I clean the table.
11. I take my notebook.
12. I go to school/work.

■ *action sequence* ➡
every evening

1. I come home.
2. I'm hungry.
3. I cook dinner.
4. I eat.
5. I clean up the kitchen.
6. I relax.
7. I call my friend.
8. I study English.
9. I watch TV.
10. I put my children to bed.
11. I get tired.
12. I go to the bedroom.
13. I take off my clothes.
14. I go to the bathroom.
15. I take a shower.
16. I go back to the bedroom.
17. I go to bed.

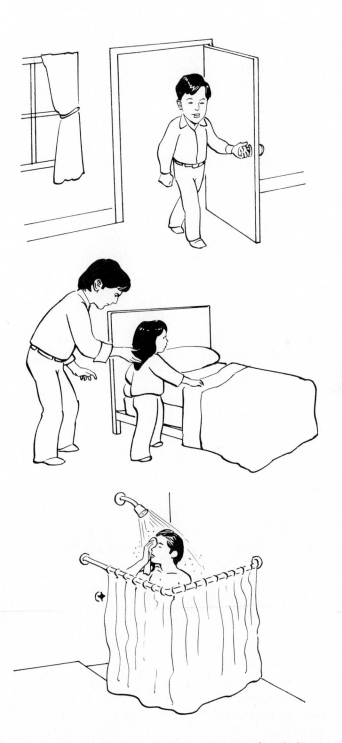

What Time Is It?

Study.

clock

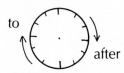

to   after

watch

It's 4:00.
It's four o'clock.

It's 4:05.
It's five (minutes) after four.

It's 4:15.
It's quarter after four.

It's 4:20.
It's twenty after four.

It's 4:30.
It's half past four.

It's 4:35.
It's twenty-five to five.

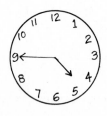

It's 4:45.
It's quarter to five.

It's 4:58.
It's two minutes to five.

It's 5:00.
It's five o'clock.

A.M. = morning
P.M. = afternoon

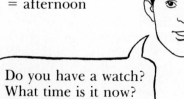

Do you have a watch?
What time is it now?

*Look at your watch.
Then draw the hands
and write the time.*

_____

_____

What Time Do You —?

Read these questions.

What time do you   get up?
                              eat breakfast?
                              leave home?
                              take the bus?
                              get to school/work?
                              start class/work?
                              leave school/work?
                              get home?
                              eat lunch?
                              eat dinner?
                              go to bed?

Now write the times.

1. I get up at _____.

2. I eat breakfast at _____.

3. I leave home at _____.

4. I take the bus at _____.

5. I get to school/work at _____.

6. I start class/work at _____.

7. I leave school/work at _____.

8. I get home at _____.

9. I eat lunch at _____.

10. I eat dinner at _____.

11. I go to bed at _____.

leave home

take the bus

get to school

start class

leave school

get home

Now practice these questions with another student.

EATING

Study these words.

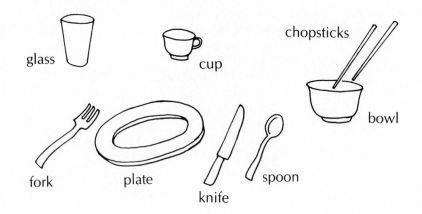

COOKING

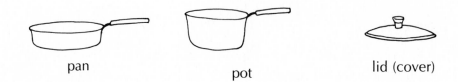

WASHING AND CLEANING

structure practice

Study.

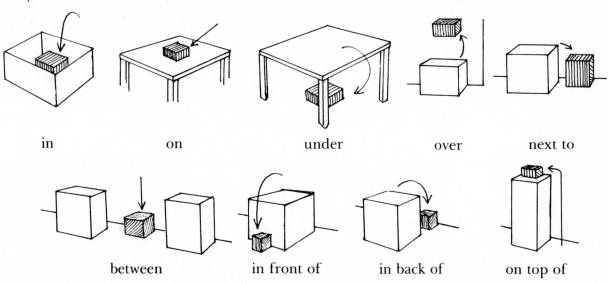

in	on	under	over	next to

between	in front of	in back of	on top of

Look at the picture and write the answers and the questons. Use contractions.

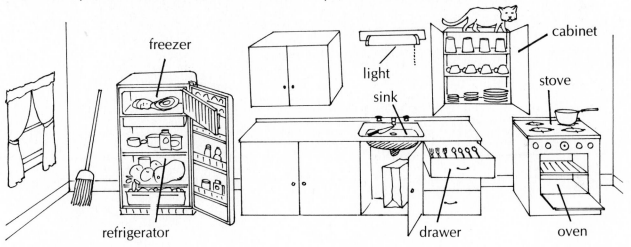

freezer

cabinet

light

stove

sink

refrigerator

drawer

oven

1. Where are the cups?   <u>They're in the cabinet.</u>

2. Where are the spoons?   _____

3. Where is the pot?   _____

4. Where is the food?   _____

5. Where is the knife?   _____

6. Where is the garbage bag?   _____

7. _____   They're in the cabinet.

8. _____   It's over the sink.

9. _____   It's next to the refrigerator.

10. _____   It's on top of the cabinet.

Now practice with another student.

SELF-TEST

A *Write the correct word under the picture.*

1. _____   2. _____   3. _____   4. _____   5. _____

6. _____   7. _____   8. _____   9. _____   10. _____

11. _____   12. _____   13. _____   14. _____   15. _____

B *Look at the picture and answer the questions.*

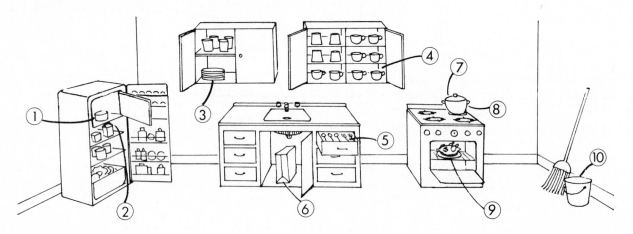

1. Where is the meat?   <u>It's in the freezer.</u> _____

2. Where is the milk? _____

3. Where are the plates? _____

4. Where are the cups? _____

5. Where are the spoons? _____

6. Where is the garbage bag? _____

7. Where is the pot? _____

8. Where is the lid? _____

9. Where is the chicken? _____

10. Where is the bucket? _____

FOOD

Study these words.

Drinks

| water | coffee | tea | milk | juice | soft drinks | beer |

Fruit

| apple | orange | lemon | banana | pineapple | strawberries | grapes |

Vegetables

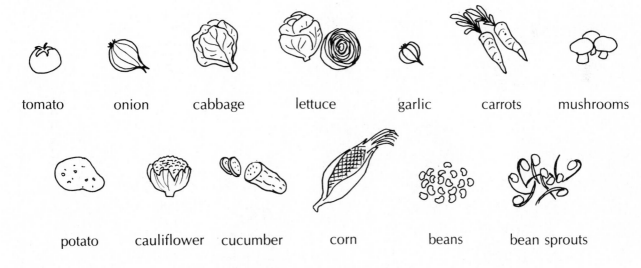

| tomato | onion | cabbage | lettuce | garlic | carrots | mushrooms |

| potato | cauliflower | cucumber | corn | beans | bean sprouts |

Meat

| beef | pork | chicken | egg |

Seafood

fish

shrimp

rice   bread   noodles

sugar   salt   pepper   oil

soy sauce   fish sauce   hot peppers

Do you like spicy food?

WATER!

AMERICAN MEALS

Study these words.

Breakfast

orange juice, coffee, bread (toast), butter, fried eggs, bacon, milk, sugar, CORN FLAKES, cereal, sweet roll, donut

Lunch

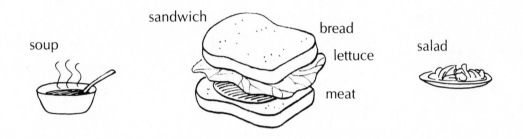

soup, sandwich, bread, lettuce, meat, salad

Dinner

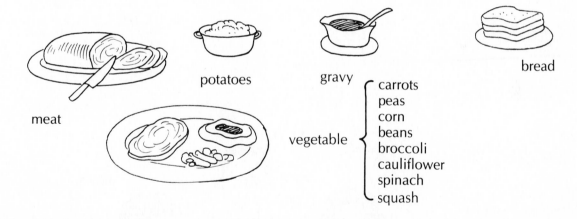

meat, potatoes, gravy, bread, vegetable

- carrots
- peas
- corn
- beans
- broccoli
- cauliflower
- spinach
- squash

Dessert

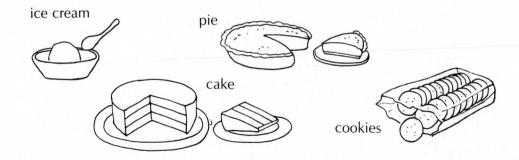

ice cream, pie, cake, cookies

■ *action sequence* ➡
frying chicken

1. Open the refrigerator.
2. Look for the chicken.
3. Take it out.
4. Wash the chicken.
5. Cut it.
6. Put the pan on the stove.
7. Put some oil in the pan.
8. Turn on the fire.
9. When the oil is hot, put the chicken in the pan.
10. Fry the chicken. It smells good!
11. Turn it over.
12. When it's finished cooking, turn off the stove.
13. Take out the chicken.
14. Eat it. It tastes good!
15. Clean the stove.

It smells good.

It looks good.

It tastes good.

How do you fry chicken? Explain to your class.

Read and discuss.

In America we buy food at a food store. A big food store is a *supermarket*. Supermarkets sell many kinds of food: fruit, vegetables, meat, bread, milk, canned foods, drinks. They also sell soap, paper towels, aspirin, and many other things.

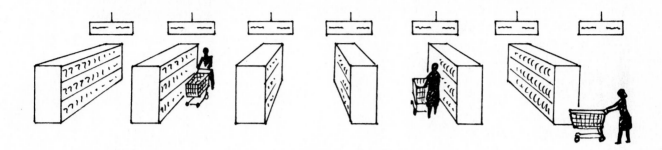

■ action sequence ➡
going shopping

1. Go in the store.
2. Take a *shopping cart*.
3. Walk through the store.
4. Read the *signs* in the *aisles*.
5. Look for the food you want to buy.
6. Put the food in the cart.
7. Go to the *checkout counter*.
8. Put your food on the counter.
9. Pay the cashier.

If you don't have a lot of things to buy, you can go to the *Express Line*.

Finding Things in the Supermarket

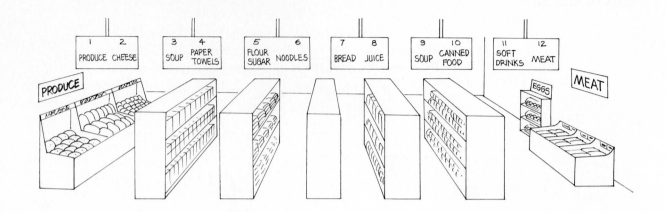

Practice this conversation.

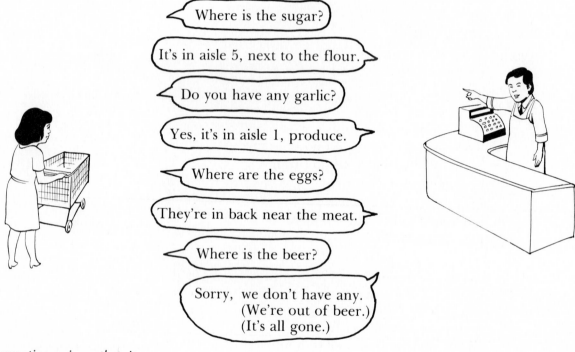

Where is the sugar?

It's in aisle 5, next to the flour.

Do you have any garlic?

Yes, it's in aisle 1, produce.

Where are the eggs?

They're in back near the meat.

Where is the beer?

Sorry, we don't have any.
(We're out of beer.)
(It's all gone.)

Now practice using other items.

structure practice

Study.

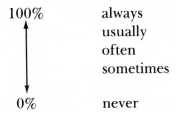

100%	always
	usually
	often
	sometimes
0%	never

I *always* go shopping at Food Mart.
I *usually* go shopping at Food Mart.
I *often* go shopping at Food Mart.
Sometimes I go shopping at Food Mart.
I go shopping at Food Mart *sometimes*.
I *never* go shopping at Food Mart.

A *Make sentences using the above words.*

1. eat breakfast at 7:00   I usually eat breakfast at 7:00.
2. watch TV after dinner   _____
3. study English at night   _____
4. wash clothes on Saturday   _____
5. eat a hamburger for lunch   _____
6. drink coffee in the morning   _____
7. eat fresh fruit for breakfast _____
8. use chopsticks   _____
9. take a shower in the afternoon _____
10. go to the movies downtown   _____

B *Complete the sentences.*

1. I always _____
2. I usually _____
3. I often _____
4. Sometimes I _____
5. I never _____

structure practice

Study.

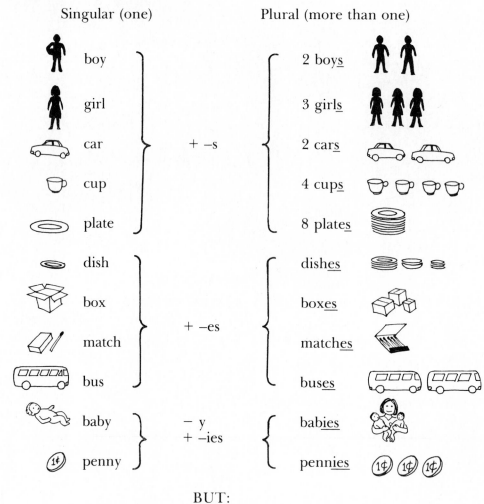

Singular (one)   Plural (more than one)

boy   2 boy<u>s</u>
girl   3 girl<u>s</u>
car   + –s   2 car<u>s</u>
cup   4 cup<u>s</u>
plate   8 plate<u>s</u>

dish   dish<u>es</u>
box   box<u>es</u>
match   + –es   match<u>es</u>
bus   bus<u>es</u>

baby   – y   bab<u>ies</u>
penny   + –ies   penn<u>ies</u>

BUT:

child   children
man   men
woman   women
foot   feet
tooth   teeth

Write the plural. Then read each column and pronounce carefully.

1. brother _____	9. pot _____	17. watch _____
2. friend _____	10. book _____	18. glass _____
3. day _____	11. mop _____	19. house _____
4. dollar _____	12. fork _____	20. box _____
5. bag _____	13. minute _____	21. page _____
6. apple _____	14. stamp _____	22. piece _____
7. lady _____	15. cabinet _____	23. size _____
8. eye _____	16. sink _____	24. brush _____

CONTAINERS

Study these words.

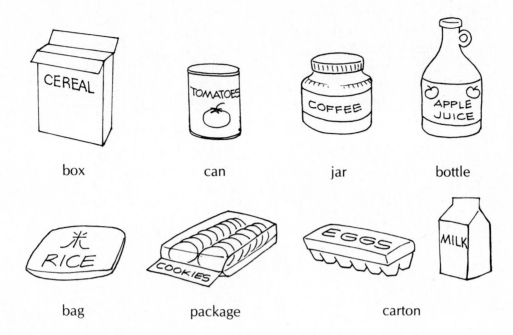

box   can   jar   bottle

bag   package   carton

Look at the pictures and fill in the blanks.

1. A box of _cereal_____
2. A can of _____
3. A _____ __ _____
4. __ _____ __ _____

5. __ _____ __ _____
6. __ _____ __ _____
7. __ _____ __ _____
8. __ _____ __ _____

  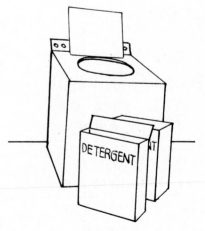

9. ___three___ ___bottles___ 10. _____ _____ 11. _____ _____
  ___of___ ___oil___   ___ _____   ___ _____

SELF-TEST

A *Which aisle?*

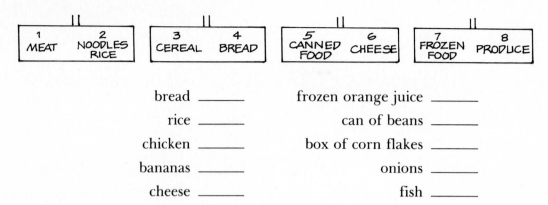

bread _____   frozen orange juice _____

rice _____   can of beans _____

chicken _____   box of corn flakes _____

bananas _____   onions _____

cheese _____   fish _____

B *Fill in the blanks.*

<u>a</u> <u>jar</u> _____ _____ _____ _____

<u>of</u> _____ _____ _____

<u>pickles</u> _____ _____ _____ _____

C *Circle "right" or "wrong."*

1.	right	wrong	I eat soup with a knife.
2.	right	wrong	Put meat and vegetables in the refrigerator.
3.	right	wrong	Wash food before you eat it.
4.	right	wrong	Vegetables are good to eat.
5.	right	wrong	Sugar is bad for your teeth.
6.	right	wrong	If I buy a lot of things in the supermarket, I can go to the Express Line.

D *Put these actions in order.*

_____ Look at the aisle signs.

_____ Put the food in the cart.

_1_ Take a shopping cart.

_____ Pay the cashier.

_____ Go to the checkout counter.

_____ Take the food you want.

Fast Food Restaurants

Many Americans like to eat at "fast food" restaurants because they are fast and cheap.

HAMBURGER	.70	SOFT DRINKS	40/.50/.60
CHEESEBURGER	.80	MILK SHAKE	.85
FISH SANDWICH	1.10	COFFEE	.35/.50
FRENCH FRIES	.60	MILK	.40
LARGE FRIES	.80	ORANGE JUICE	.50

Practice these conversations.

1. *Girl:* May I help you?
   Boy: Give me a hamburger, fries, and a small coke, please.
   Girl: Is that for here or to go?
   Boy: For here.
   Girl: That's $1.81.

2. *Girl:* May I take your order?
   Boy: Large fries, please.
   Girl: Is that all?
   Boy: Yes, that's all.
   Girl: Just a minute; they're not ready yet.

hamburger

cheeseburger

straw   lid

napkin   cup

fried potatoes (French fries)

tray

small medium large

listening and speaking

A *Listen to your teacher pronounce these words. Then listen again and repeat. Then listen to your teacher pronounce the key words below, and write under them the words that have the same sound in the same position. Check the word after you use it (✓); use some words twice (✓) (✓).*

rice ( )   use (verb) ( )   beef ( )( )
mop ( )   pot ( )( )   peas ( )( )( )
bowl ( )   house ( )

1	2	3	4	5	6
<u>p</u>an	<u>b</u>ook	gla<u>ss</u>	si<u>z</u>e	h<u>o</u>t	<u>ea</u>t

_____   _____   _____   _____   _____   _____

_____   _____   _____   _____   _____   _____

Now think, and write one more word for each number.

_____   _____   _____   _____   _____   _____

B *Circle the cluster and pronounce.*

store	spoon	sponge	sprouts
straw	squash	sweet	shrimp
plate	plastic	glass	class
clock	clean	cream	broom
bread	fry	fruit	frozen
flour	drink	drain	tray
three	through		

pan / fan   pan / pen
put / foot   man / men
pork / fork   bad / bed

right / light   it / eat
wrong / long   his / he's
                 live / leave
rice / right
nice / night / knife

PRACTICE THESE WORDS

C *Your teacher will pronounce these words. Listen and repeat.*

_ ´   _ ´ _   ´ _ _   _ _ _ ´

ca shier   ba na na   ham bur ger   af ter noon
                   po ta to   straw ber ry
                                      veg é ta ble

´ _ _ _   _ _ ´ _ _ _

su per mar ket   re fri ge ra tor

Now pronounce these words and write them above in the correct column:

detergent   wastebasket   packages

Housing

chapter three

COMPETENCIES:

1. Give information about one's living situation
2. Recognize and describe problems in house or apartment
3. Talk to landlord about problems
4. Take care of housing: sanitation, maintenance, safety
5. Read signs for rentals
6. Ask about housing for rent
7. Fill out a simple rental application form

ORIENTATION:

1. American family structure and relationships
2. Housing in America: types of housing, rental procedures and conditions, expectations
3. Care of housing: sanitation, maintenance, and safety

STRUCTURES:

1. Present tense of *do* verbs: affirmative, negative, interrogative, short answers, *wh*-questions
2. Object pronouns
3. *There is/are:* affirmative, negative, interrogative
4. Noun modifiers

Teacher Notes and Suggestions

Page 44
1. Read the story to the class and ask comprehension questions. Read it again, have students repeat it. Then point out third person singular formations, including question formation.
2. Explain that house or apartment size is measured in number of bedrooms.

Pages 46 to 48
Structures should be presented and thoroughly practiced orally first. These pages serve as summarization and reinforcement.

Page 49
1. Explain family relationships beginning with Jerry and working out. It should be explained to students of certain language groups, particularly Asianic, that English does not distinguish between *older* and *younger* brothers or sisters or aunts or uncles.
2. Activity: Have a student come to the front of the class and introduce him- or herself. Then bring up another student as his wife/her husband. One by one add family members from the class, frequently asking various members of the "family," "Who's he?" ("He's my uncle"); and asking of the class while pointing to two members, "Who's she?" ("She's his sister-in-law"). Then have the class ask such questions of the family.

Page 50
Introduce the topic by reviewing, "Who do you live with?" and speak in your own words about family life. Then read the page and have the students follow. Follow suggested procedure for Orientation Notes (see page *ix*).

Page 51
"Show me (him, her, them, us) your watch," and passing an object around with the words "Give it to me (etc.)" are good ways to introduce and practice object pronouns.

Page 52
Discuss living accommodations of students—rooms, furnishings, and so on—now and in their native countries. Then use the picture to present the vocabulary. Have students number items in each room. Practice vocabulary further using prepositions of position, such as "The lamp is on the table," "The table is next to the armchair," "Where is the coffee table?" ("In front of the sofa").

Page 53
1. Introduce and discuss the topic. Relate it to the situation in students' native countries. Read and practice as suggested.
2. Point out the use and meaning of *have to*.

Page 54
Introduce structure by setting up objects in the classroom in a cabinet or on a table and having students practice questions and answers with "Is/Are there . . . ?" Then ask students questions about their apartment or house, such as "Is there a rug in your bedroom?" and have them practice such questions among themselves.

Page 55
Present narrative page as suggested. Point out the use of noun modifiers (e.g., "bathroom sink").

Page 56
Use pictures to present vocabulary. Note stress differences in various combination words.

Page 57
Present and practice material; have pair practice with "What's wrong?" Ask students what problems they have in their apartment.

Page 58
After practicing conversation A as suggested (see page *ix*), have students write their own dialogue. They may work in small groups, in pairs, or individually. Have students present their dialogue to the class.

Page 60
Present Action Sequence as suggested.

Page 62
Introduce the page by talking about looking for a place to live, noting that a common way is to look for signs. Study and discuss signs; point out special vocabulary and explain the meanings of the abbreviations. Note relation of price to type and size of accommodation.

Page 63	Follow the suggested procedure for presentation and practice.
Page 64	1. Read while students listen and follow. Ask comprehension questions. Later students may practice reading. 2. Point out structure *have to*.
Page 65	Practice filling out the form as a group first, line by line or section by section. Explain all necessary details.

Jerry's Apartment

Read and discuss.

Jerry Morton lives at 2240 Dale Street. He lives with his family in a one-bedroom apartment. The rent is $220. Four people live in the apartment: Jerry, his wife Diane, and their two children.

Jerry doesn't like the apartment because it's small and old. It's near the bus stop, but it's far from downtown and it's far from the supermarket.

Answer these questions.

1. Where does Jerry live?
2. Who does he live with?
3. How many bedrooms does the apartment have?
4. How much is the rent?
5. How many people live in the apartment?
6. Does Jerry like his apartment? Why?
7. Is the apartment near downtown?

Now answer these questions for yourself. Then practice with another student.

1. Where do you live?
2. Do you live in a house or an apartment?
3. How many bedrooms does it have? (How big is it?)
4. How much is the rent? (What's the rent?)
5. Who do you live with?
6. Do you like your apartment (your house)? Why?

structure practice

Study.

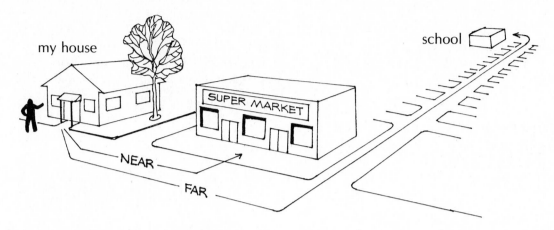

The supermarket is *near* my house.
My house is *near* the supermarket.

The school is *far* from my house.
My house is *far* from the school.

A *Look at the picture and fill in the blanks.*

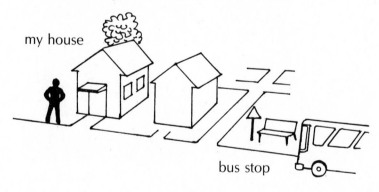

1. The bus stop is _____ my house.

2. My house is _____ from downtown.

3. My house is _____ the bus stop.

4. Downtown is _____ from my house.

B *Answer these questions and practice with another student.*

1. Is your house near downtown?
2. Is the bus stop near your house?
3. Is your house near the supermarket?
4. Is the school far from your house?

structure practice

A *Study these verbs.*

					AND:	BUT:
I	live	he	lives		wash - washes	have - has
you	speak	she	speaks		fix - fixes	do - does
we	etc.	it	etc.		etc.	go - goes
they						
					study - studies	
					carry - carries	
					etc.	

Examples:

1. I *speak* English.
2. They *live* in the United States.
3. She *wants* a job.
4. Jerry *has* a big family.

Fill in the blanks, using the correct form.

(speak) 1. I ____speak____ English.

(take) 2. We _____ the bus.

(like) 3. She _____ America.

(have) 4. They _____ a nice house.

(work) 5. Jerry _____ downtown.

(go) 6. His wife _____ to English class.

B *Study the negative.*

I		he	
you		she	
we	don't live	it	doesn't live
they	speak		speak
	etc.		etc.

Examples:

1. I *don't speak* English.
2. They *don't live* in the United States.
3. She *doesn't want* a job.
4. Jerry *doesn't have* a big family.

Change the sentences in Part A above to negative.

1. _____

2. _____

3. _____

4. _____

5. _____

6. _____

C *Study the questions.*

Do $\left\{\begin{array}{l} \text{I} \\ \text{you} \\ \text{we} \\ \text{they} \end{array}\right\}$ live . . . ?
speak
etc.

Does $\left\{\begin{array}{l} \text{he} \\ \text{she} \\ \text{it} \end{array}\right\}$ live . . . ?
speak
etc.

Examples:

1. *Do* you *speak* English?
2. *Do* they *live* in the United States?
3. *Does* she *want* a job?
4. *Does* Jerry *have* a big family?

Look at the answers and write the questions.

1. _____   Yes, I live near school.

2. _____ Jerry_____   Yes, he works downtown.

3. _____   No, we don't take the bus.

4. _____   Yes, they have a nice house.

5. _____ your daughter_____   No, she doesn't understand English.

D *Study these examples. Then practice with another student.*

Questions	Answers	Short answers
1. Do you like your apartment?	-Yes, I like my apartment. -No, I don't like my apartment.	-Yes, I do. -No, I don't.
2. Do they want to move?	-Yes, they want to move. -No, they don't want to move.	-Yes, they do. -No, they don't.
3. Does Jerry have a car?	-Yes, he has a car. -No, he doesn't have a car.	-Yes, he does. -No, he doesn't.
4. Does your mother live with you?	-Yes, she lives with me. -No, she doesn't live with me.	-Yes, she does. -No, she doesn't.

E *Study these examples.*

1. *Where* do you live?   - (I live) in Oak Park.
2. *What* do you eat for lunch?   - (I eat) a sandwich.
3. *When* does she have class?   - (She has class) every morning.
4. *How* does Jerry go to work?   - He drives.
5. *What time* do your children go to bed?   - (They go to bed) at 9:00.

Now look at the answers and write the questions.

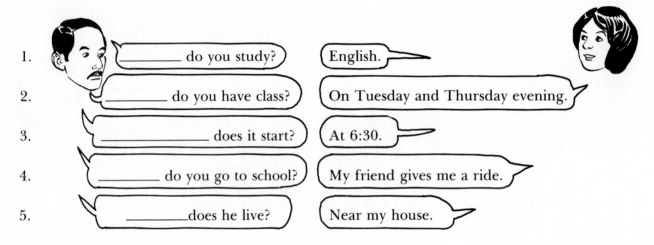

1. _____ do you study?   English.
2. _____ do you have class?   On Tuesday and Thursday evening.
3. _____ does it start?   At 6:30.
4. _____ do you go to school?   My friend gives me a ride.
5. _____ does he live?   Near my house.

F *Complete the conversation. Then practice with another student.*

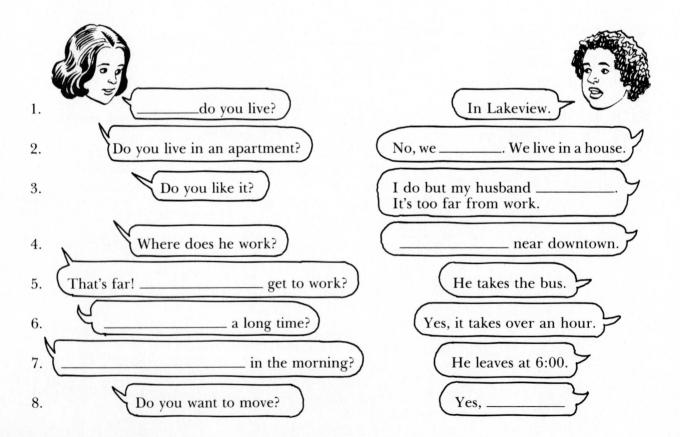

1. _____ do you live?   In Lakeview.
2. Do you live in an apartment?   No, we _____. We live in a house.
3. Do you like it?   I do but my husband _____. It's too far from work.
4. Where does he work?   _____ near downtown.
5. That's far! _____ get to work?   He takes the bus.
6. _____ a long time?   Yes, it takes over an hour.
7. _____ in the morning?   He leaves at 6:00.
8. Do you want to move?   Yes, _____

FAMILY

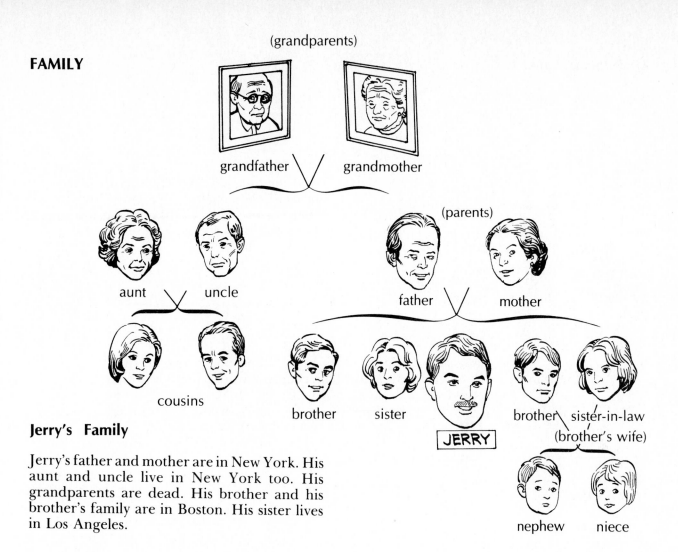

Jerry's Family

Jerry's father and mother are in New York. His aunt and uncle live in New York too. His grandparents are dead. His brother and his brother's family are in Boston. His sister lives in Los Angeles.

Diane's Family

Diane's family is in Texas.

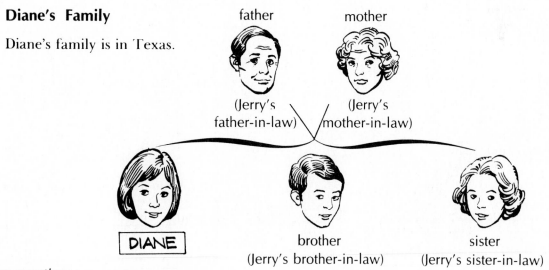

Answer these questions.

1. Where are Jerry's parents?
2. Where does his brother live?
3. Where does his sister live?
4. Where is Diane's family?

Read and discuss.

In America usually only a husband and wife and their children live together in the same house. Other relatives—parents, brothers and sisters, aunts and uncles and cousins—live in different houses. Sometimes they talk to each other on the telephone or see each other on weekends or holidays.

Americans usually don't have a lot of children—one or two or three, or none. Usually when children are about twenty years old, they leave their parents' house and live alone or with their friends. Sometimes they go away to study, or they get married. They visit their parents and brothers and sisters, but they like to live alone and take care of themselves.

When the children get married or go away, the parents live alone. Usually old people don't want to live with their children, because they like to take care of themselves, but they like to live near their children.

When they are very old or sick, many people go to live in a nursing home or in a home for old people.

structure practice

A *Study and practice.*

I / me	he / him	we / us
you / you	she / her	they / them
	it / it	

Examples:

1. I like *you.*
2. You like *me.*
3. I like *him.*
4. He likes *me.*
5. He likes *her.*
6. She likes *him.*
7. We like *them.*
8. They like *us.*

9. I like Jerry./I like *him.*
10. I like Diane./I like *her.*
11. I like Jerry and Diane./I like *them.*
12. I like my apartment./I like *it.*
13. I like the curtains./I like *them.*
14. Tell *me (him/her/them/us).*
15. Show *me (him/her/them/us).*
16. Give it to *me (him/her/them/us).*

B *Finish the sentence.*

1. I like her, and __she likes me_____.
2. I like her, but __she doesn't like me_____.
3. She likes him, and _____.
4. We visit them, and _____.
5. He writes to her, but _____.
6. I know you, but _____.

C *Write the answer, using pronouns. Then practice.*

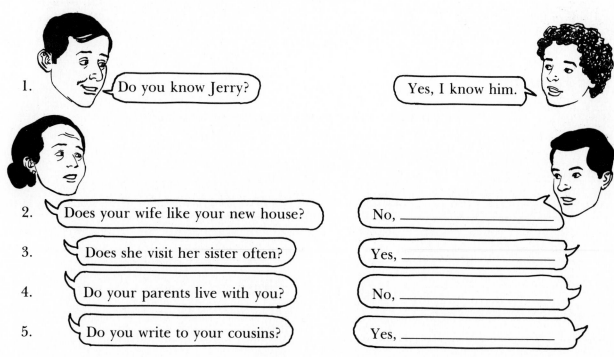

1. Do you know Jerry? — Yes, I know him.

2. Does your wife like your new house? — No, _____

3. Does she visit her sister often? — Yes, _____

4. Do your parents live with you? — No, _____

5. Do you write to your cousins? — Yes, _____

Rooms and Furniture

Study the picture, then number each item in the picture.

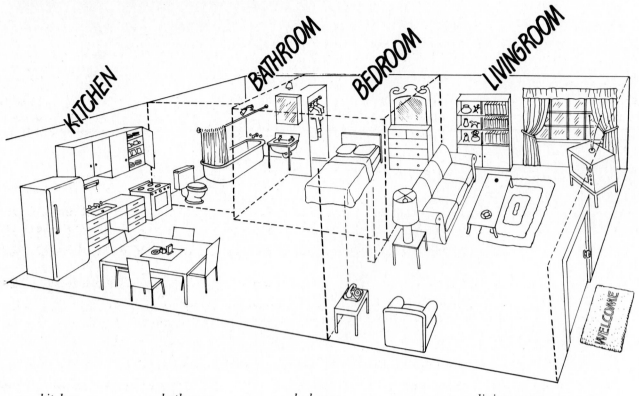

kitchen	*bathroom*	*bedroom*	*living room*	
1. refrigerator	7. bathtub	12. bed	16. sofa	21. rug
2. sink	8. shower	13. pillows	17. shelves	22. coffee table
3. cabinets	9. sink (washbowl)	14. dresser (chest)	18. window	23. ashtray
4. stove	10. mirror	15. closet	19. curtains	24. armchair
5. kitchen table	11. toilet		20. television	25. lamp
6. chairs				

Your Furniture

What do you have in your house or apartment?

kitchen		bathroom	
stove	_____	sink	_____
_____	_____	_____	_____
_____	_____	_____	_____

living room		bedroom	
sofa	_____	bed	_____
_____	_____	_____	_____
_____	_____	_____	_____
_____			

Answer these questions and practice with another student.

1. Does your apartment have curtains? What color are they?
2. Do you have a rug in your living room? What color is it?
3. Do you have a closet in your bedroom?
4. Where do you put your clothes?
5. What do you need for your apartment?
6. Do you like to take a shower or a bath?
7. Do you have a gas stove or an electric stove?
8. How many doors does your apartment have?

Orientation Notes: HOUSES AND APARTMENTS

Read and discuss.

 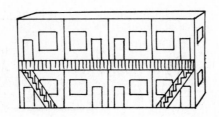 

Some Americans live in houses, some live in apartments. Houses and apartments have one, two, three, or more bedrooms. Usually only one or two people sleep in one bedroom.

It's very expensive to buy a house. Many people rent apartments or houses. They pay rent every month to a *landlord (manager).* If you rent you usually need to buy *furniture.* You pay for the telephone and for *gas* and *electricity.*

You have to be quiet in an apartment. You have to clean it and take care of it. Talk to the landlord if you have problems.

Americans often don't know the *neighbors.* If you don't know your neighbors, go talk to them. They think you don't speak English.

If you don't like your apartment, or if it's expensive, you can move. Look around for another apartment, or ask your friends. Look in the newspaper.

structure practice

Study and practice.

Examples:

1. *There is (There's)* a rug in the bedroom.
2. *There is (There's)* a window in the kitchen.
3. *There are* curtains in the bathroom.
4. *There are* cups in the cabinet.

Questions	Short answers	
5. *Is there* a rug in the bedroom?	-Yes, *there is.*	-No, *there isn't.*
6. *Is there* a window in the kitchen?	-Yes, *there is.*	-No, *there isn't.*
7. *Are there* (any) curtains in the bathroom?	-Yes, *there are.*	-No, *there aren't* (any).
8. *Are there* (any) cups in the cabinet?	-Yes, *there are.*	-No, *there aren't* (any).

A Answer these questions about your house or apartment. Write the short answer. Then practice with another student.

1. Is there a rug in your living room? _____

2. Are there curtains? _____

3. Is there a lot of furniture? _____

4. Are there a lot of cabinets? _____

5. Is there a closet in the bedroom? _____

6. Are there shelves in the living room? _____

B Look at the picture and complete the questions and answers.

1. (Are there any cups?) There are (some) cups in the cabinet.

2. (_____ any forks?) _____ in the drawer.

3. (_____ any glasses?) _____ in the sink.

4. (_____ any bread?) _____ in the refrigerator.

4. (_____ any beer?) Sorry, _____

Inside Jerry's Apartment

Read and discuss.

Jerry's apartment is small and old. It's in bad *condition*. The stove is old and the refrigerator door is broken. There are a lot of cockroaches. The bathroom sink leaks and the toilet is noisy. Jerry calls the landlord, but the landlord doesn't do anything.

There aren't any curtains, and the rug is old and dirty. Jerry has a little furniture, but he needs a sofa and a lamp and one more bed.

Answer these questions.

1. How is Jerry's apartment?
2. What's wrong with the apartment?
3. Does Jerry talk to the landlord?
4. What does the landlord do?
5. Is there a rug in the apartment?
6. Are there curtains?
7. Does Jerry have much furniture?
8. What does he need for his apartment?

structure practice

A *Study and complete.*

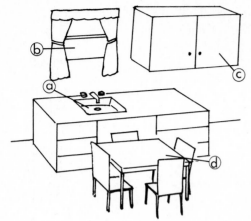

a. kitchen sink
b. kitchen window
c. kitchen _____
d. _____ _____

What do you call . . . ?

1. the table in the kitchen   _____
2. the sink in the bathroom   _____
3. the window in the bedroom   _____
4. the faucet in the bathtub   _____
5. the door of the refrigerator   _____

Now read the combination words. Pronounce them with equal stress: ⎯́⎯ ⎯́⎯.

B *Study.*

| lamp for the floor
= floor lamp | lamp for the wall
= wall lamp | lamp for a table
= table lamp | table for a lamp
= lamp table |

What do you call . . . ?

1. a cup for coffee   _____   5. a dish for soap   _____
2. a table for coffee   _____   6. a cabinet for
    medicine   _____
3. a bag for garbage   _____   7. a curtain for
    the shower   _____
4. a pan for frying   _____   8. a lock on a door   _____

Pronounce these combination words ⎯́⎯ ⎯⎯⎯.

C *Some combination words are written together. What do these words mean?*

1. toothbrush   a brush for teeth _____
2. dishtowel   _____
3. bookshelf   _____
4. bathtub   _____
5. armchair   _____

Pronounce these combination words. ⎯́⎯ ⎯⎯⎯.

Apartment Problems

Study and practice.

1. The _____ is leaking.

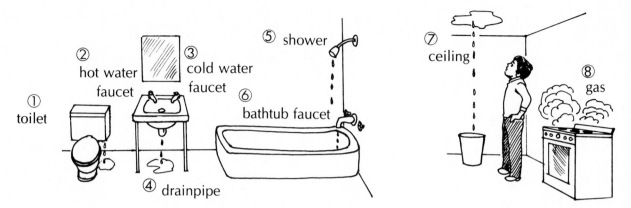

- ① toilet
- ② hot water faucet
- ③ cold water faucet
- ⑤ shower
- ⑥ bathtub faucet
- ④ drainpipe
- ⑦ ceiling
- ⑧ gas

2. The _____ is stopped up.

- ① kitchen sink
- ② toilet
- ③ bathroom sink
- ④ bathtub

3. The _____ doesn't work.

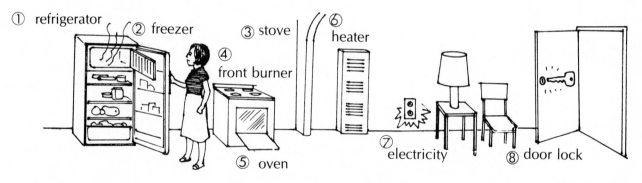

- ① refrigerator
- ② freezer
- ③ stove
- ④ front burner
- ⑤ oven
- ⑥ heater
- ⑦ electricity
- ⑧ door lock

4. The _____ is broken.

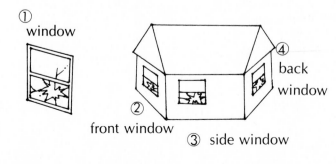

- ① window
- ② front window
- ③ side window
- ④ back window

5. There are _____ in my apartment.

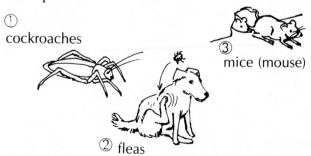

- ① cockroaches
- ② fleas
- ③ mice (mouse)

Calling the Landlord

A *Practice this conversation.*

Hello. This is Jerry Morton on Dale Street. May I speak to the landlord, Mr. Wilson?

This is Mr. Wilson.

I have a problem in my apartment.

What's wrong?

The bathroom sink is leaking. Can you come and fix it?

How bad is it?

Not too bad, but there's water on the floor.

Put a pan under the sink, and I'll fix it tomorrow.

The toilet is noisy, too, and the refrigrator door is broken.

OK, I'll take a look tomorrow.

What time can you come?

In the morning, around 9:00.

Thank you very much. See you tomorrow.

B *Now write a conversation. Call your landlord and tell him about a problem in your apartment.*

Orientation Notes: TAKING CARE OF YOUR HOUSE

Read and discuss.

Cleaning the house

1. Sweep and mop the floor.
2. *Vacuum* the rugs.
3. Wash the bathroom with strong soap.

Taking care of the kitchen

1. Keep the stove and sink clean.
2. *Defrost* the freezer when it has a lot of ice. Don't use a knife!
3. Don't leave the refrigerator door open a long time.
4. Don't use the oven to heat your house.
5. If you smell gas, check the stove and water heater. Maybe the *pilot light* is out.

Taking care of drains

1. Don't put food or oil down the drain.
2. If you have a *garbage disposal,* you can put soft food in it. First turn on the water, then turn on the garbage disposal. Be careful! Don't put bones in it. Don't put your hand in it.
3. Don't let hair go down the bathtub drain.
4. Clean slow drains with *drain cleaner.*
5. Open stopped drains with a *plunger.*

Fighting *insects*

1. Don't leave food open. Close bags and boxes of food.
2. Close your garbage bag.
3. Use *insect spray* to kill insects.

If you have any problems, talk to the landlord.

spraying for insects

1. Buy *insect spray* or *bug killer*.
2. Read the directions on the can.
3. Move the dishes out of your cabinets.
4. Move your food out of the room.
5. Spray your kitchen—in the cabinets, behind the stove, under the refrigerator, around the floor.
6. Spray everywhere you see bugs.
7. Wash the cabinets.
8. Put the spray away in a high cabinet.

Be careful! It's poison.

Don't spray food or dishes.
Don't spray things your children touch.
Don't breathe in the spray.

Don't spray near fire.
Don't smoke when you spray.

Remember:

Clean your kitchen.
Put food away.
Close your garbage bag.

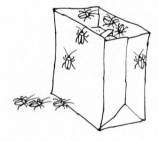

SELF-TEST

A *Draw a line and complete the sentences.*

1. If you don't like your apartment   you have to clean it
2. If you don't know your neighbors   talk to the landlord
3. If your apartment is dirty   you can move
4. If you want to find an apartment   you have to be quiet
5. If you live in an apartment   go talk to them
6. If you have problems with your apartment   look around or ask your friends

B *Look at the pictures and fill in the blanks.*

What's wrong?

1. _____   3. _____

2. _____   4. _____

C *Fill in the blanks.*

1. I want to sweep the floor. Go get me the _____.
2. I want to mop the floor. Go get me the _____.
3. The rugs are dirty. Go get the _____.
4. This drain is stopped up. Go get the _____.
5. This drain is slow. Go get me the _____.
6. There are a lot of insects in here. Go get the _____ _____.

D *Good or bad?*

___good___ 1. I keep the bathroom clean.

_____ 2. I close my garbage bag every night.

_____ 3. I spray for insects in my baby's bed.

_____ 4. I put the bug killer away in a high cabinet.

_____ 5. I put my old food down the drain.

"For Rent" Signs

Read these signs and answer the questions.

How much is the rent?

Does the apartment take children?

How many bedrooms
does the apartment have?

Who can I talk to
about this apartment?

When can I move in?

Is the apartment available now?

Looking for an Apartment

Read and practice.

Jerry wants to move, and he goes to look for a new apartment. He knocks on the landlord's door.

Landlord: Yes?

Jerry: Hello. Do you have an apartment for rent?

Landlord: Yes, I do.

Jerry: How many bedrooms does it have?

Landlord: Two.

Jerry: What's the rent?

Landlord: $285. How many people are there?

Jerry: Four. Can I see the apartment?

Landlord: Sure. Just a second . . . Where do you work?

Jerry: I work at the Best Box Company.

Landlord: This is the apartment. You pay gas and electricity. There's a $250 deposit.

Jerry: Can I get the deposit back?

Landlord: Yes, if you pay your rent and leave the apartment clean.

Jerry: Is there a lease?

Landlord: No, just the deposit.

Jerry: When can I move in?

Landlord: On the first of the month.

Jerry: OK. I'll take it.

Landlord: All right. Your first payment is $535—$250 deposit plus the first month's rent.

Read and discuss.

Rent

1. You have to pay the rent every month, usually on the first day of the month. Pay on time. Don't pay late.
2. Pay cash or pay by check or money order. Get a *receipt*.
3. The *landlord (manager)* can raise your rent. He has to tell you one month before.
4. Sometimes you have to pay more rent if a lot of people live in your apartment.
5. Most apartments are unfurnished, but they have a stove and a refrigerator. In a few apartments you have to buy or rent a stove and refrigerator. Furnished apartments have more furniture and you have to pay more rent.

Deposit

1. You have to pay a *deposit* before you move in.
2. The landlord gives you back your deposit when you move away.
3. The landlord can keep your deposit money if you move away and you don't pay the rent, or you break something, or your apartment is very dirty, or you don't tell the landlord 30 days before you move.

Utilities and telephone

1. *Utilities* are gas and electric service.
2. Sometimes the landlord pays the utilities; usually you have to pay.
3. When you move in, call the gas company and the electric company to turn on your service. You usually have to pay a deposit.
4. Go to the telephone company to get a telephone for your house or apartment. You usually have to pay a deposit.

Lease

1. Some apartments have a *lease*.
2. A lease is a paper you sign when you move in. You say you will stay for one year. If you move away before one year, you can lose your deposit.

Moving

1. Tell the landlord 30 days before you move.
2. Clean your apartment.
3. Ask the landlord to give you back your deposit.
4. Tell the gas company, the electric company, the telephone company, and the post office that you are moving.

Rental Application

Sometimes when you want to move into an apartment, you have to fill out an application. Fill out this practice application.

APPLICATION TO RENT			
Name		Social Security No.	
Date of birth	Driver's License No.	State	Home phone
Present address			How long lived there
Manager's name	Mgr. phone	Reason for moving	
Previous address (your address before)			How long lived there
Manager's name	Mgr. phone	Reason for moving	

LIST OF OCCUPANTS (INCLUDE YOURSELF)			
Name	Age	Name	Age

EMPLOYMENT
Present occupation   How long worked there
Employer's name and address
Previous occupation   How long worked there
Employer's name and address

Income	Name of your bank		
$ week month	Address		Account No.

In case of emergency notify Name	Address	Phone	Relationship

Date	Signature

listening and speaking

A *Listen to your teacher pronounce these words. Then listen again and repeat. Then listen to your teacher pronounce the key words below, and write under them the words that have the same sound in the same position. Check the word after you use it (√): use some words twice (√) (√):*

they ( )   work ( )   there ( )   toilet ( )( )
room ( )   two ( )( )   rug ( )
bag ( )   poison ( )   want ( )

1	2	3	4	5	6
w<u>a</u>sh	<u>th</u>is	<u>t</u>ime	bi<u>g</u>	n<u>oi</u>sy	f<u>oo</u>d

_____   _____   _____   _____   _____   _____

_____   _____   _____   _____   _____   _____

Now think, and write one more word for each number.

_____   _____   _____   _____   _____   _____

B *Listen to the pronunciation of the final sounds. Then read each column and pronounce carefully.*

I		II		III
work<u>s</u> eat<u>s</u>		see<u>s</u> live<u>s</u>		wash<u>es</u>
like<u>s</u> want<u>s</u>		know<u>s</u> come<u>s</u>		watch<u>es</u>
speak<u>s</u> keep<u>s</u>		pay<u>s</u> call<u>s</u>		fix<u>es</u>
		ha<u>s</u> need<u>s</u>		close<u>s</u>
		studie<u>s</u> clean<u>s</u>		

C *Your teacher will pronounce these words. Listen and repeat.*

⏑ ´
re ceipt

⏑ ´ ⏑
a part ment
to ge ther
ex pen sive
con di tion

´ ⏑ ⏑
ho li day
ma na ger
re la tives
com pa ny

⏑ ⏑ ´
un der stand

´ ⏑ ⏑ ⏑
te le vi sion

⏑ ´ ⏑ ⏑
a vai la ble
Los An ge les

⏑ ⏑ ´ ⏑ ⏑
e lec tri ci ty

Now pronounce these words and write them above in the correct column:

tomorrow   furniture   deposit   utilities   newspaper

Directions and Transportation

chapter four

COMPETENCIES:

1. Ask for, understand, and give directions for getting places (walking and driving)
2. Interpret a basic map
3. Use public transportation
4. Ask for information about bus service
5. Use intercity bus

ORIENTATION:

1. Getting around in an urban setting
2. United States: map, distances
3. Transportation in America
4. City and intercity bus systems

STRUCTURES:

1. Use of preposition and article with places in *be* and *go* constructions
2. Present continuous: affirmative, negative, interrogative, short answers, *wh*-questions
3. *Going to* for future tense

Teacher Notes and Suggestions

Page 70   See suggestions on page *ix*.

Page 71
1. Words are grouped according to use with (1) no preposition *at*, and no article; (2) *at* but no *the*; (3) *at* and *the*; (4) *in* and *the* (for rooms). Group 3 may also use *in* with the meaning "inside."
2. Structure can be further practiced with words on the preceding page.

Page 73
1. Point out the use of the preposition *to* and article with places.
2. Point out the use and meaning of present continuous structure.

Page 74
1. Structure should be introduced and practiced orally first. Teacher can demonstrate actions and describe what he or she is doing using the present continuous tense.
2. Activity: Write various simple activities on cards using present continuous tense, such as "I'm cooking," "I'm watching TV," and hand out cards to students. Students act out their sentences in front of the class and the other students guess, "Are you _____ ing?" until someone guesses correctly. Then reinforce, asking "What is he/she doing?" and having the class answer. Then other students in class do what their card says for others to guess.

Page 77
1. Follow the suggested procedure for presentation and practice of dialogue (see page ix).
2. Explain special vocabulary, pointing out the difference between *in front of* and *across (the street) from*.
3. Locations in your city may be used for additional practice.

Page 78   Draw a simple street layout on the board as an example. Mark the streets and ask questions about the names of the streets and distances from street to street. Then mark a few places on the layout and have students give locations, distances, and so on. Then refer to this page; explain the layout and ask questions about it to prepare the class for the exercises.

Page 79   Follow the same type of procedure as on the preceding page. Also introduce compass directions and explain the scale of miles.

Page 80   In presenting this map, you may speak about the United States: the country, the states, the geography, the distances, and so on.

Page 82
1. Demonstrate the various operations depicted at the top of the page and direct the students to demonstrate.
2. Present and explain the map and various locations marked on it. Then read the conversation, keying it to the map. Have students practice conversations in pairs.
3. When finished, refer back to p. 77 and have students give directions for getting to various locations.

Page 83
1. Present the terms at the top of the page. Point them out in the picture.
2. Look over the picture as a group, pointing out important features. Reproduce the picture on the board, if at all possible. Introduce and practice dialogues, keying them to the picture.
3. Students can work individually or in groups to write directions for 3. To check and for further practice, have students follow on the map the directions other students give.

Page 84
1. Present and practice dialogue. Review the adverbs.
2. Students can provide variations in the dialogue from below for further practice.

Page 85 1. Present the information as suggested.
        2. Include specific information about your city's transportation systems.

Page 86 1. Follow the suggested procedure for presentation and practice.
        2. Locations and bus routes from your city may also be used.

Page 87 Practiced as suggested, with variations as desired.

Page 88 1. Explain the difference between intracity buses and intercity buses.
        2. Point out *going to* future structures.
        3. Follow the suggested procedure for presentation and practice.
        4. Ask how many students have traveled to other cities or states, and how they traveled. Compare fares to certain destinations by various means of transportation. Read the lower section and practice the conversation; point out *going to* structures. Explain ticketing and baggage check procedures. Ask questions using the picture at the bottom.

Page 89 The future with *going to* (and verb) may be confused with *going to* a place. It will have to be explained as being the same as *will* (and verb), which some students may already know, and explained as a future tense construction, illustrated by the samples shown. The conversation at the bottom should be practiced after completion.

PLACES

Study these words.

home

school

work

church

my friend's house

the store

the bank

the post office

the hospital

the doctor's office

the laundromat

the restaurant

the drugstore

the bus stop

the airport

the gas station

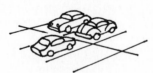
the parking lot

the park

the beach

the movies

a party

structure practice

Practice.

1. Where are they?

They're outside.   They're upstairs.   They're downtown.

2. Where is he?

He's at home.   He's at school.   He's at work.

3. Where is your wife?

She's at the store.   She's at the bank.   She's at the laundromat.

4. Where is she?

She's in the bathroom.   She's in the kitchen.   She's in the office.

Directions and Transportation   **71**

SELF-TEST

A *Fill in the blanks.*

_____She's outside._____   _____ work. _____   _____

_____   _____ home. _____   _____

B *Match.*

bank   airplanes
airport   food
gas station   stamps
laundromat   washing machines
restaurant   money
drugstore   gas
post office   medicine

C *Answer the questions.*

1. Where do you catch the bus?   at the bus stop _____
2. Where do you wash your clothes?   _____
3. Where do you see a doctor?   _____
4. Where do you see your friend?   _____
5. Where do you have a picnic?   _____
6. Where do you park your car?   in _____

72   Chapter Four

structure practice

Study and practice.

Where are you going?

I'm going home.
         outside.
         downtown.
         shopping.

I'm going to school.
        to work.
        to my friend's house.
        to Sears.
        to Los Angeles.

I'm going to the bathroom.
        to the office.
        to the store.
        to the bus stop.

Complete the sentences.

(store)   1. I'm going _____.

(work)   2. She's going _____.

(home)   3. He's going _____.

(Los Angeles)   4. We're going _____.

(shopping)   5. I'm going _____.

(bus stop)   6. They're going _____.

(airport)   7. My sister is going _____.

(movies)   8. My friends are going _____.

(inside)   9. He's going _____.

(ladies' room)   10. She's going _____.

structure practice

Study.

$$\left.\begin{array}{ll} \text{I} & \text{am} \\ \text{she} & \text{is} \\ \text{they} & \text{are} \\ & \text{etc.} \end{array}\right\} \quad \underline{\hspace{2cm}} \text{ing}$$

Examples:

1. *I am (I'm) going* home.

2. *She is (She's) eating.*

3. *They're watching* TV.

4. *He's studying.*

5. *Tom is washing* the dishes.

6. *The children are sleeping.*

A *Look at the pictures and write sentences, following the examples.*

1.  _____

2. _____

3.  _____

4. _____

B *Complete the conversations.*

1. Can I talk to Bill?

Just a minute, he's _____

2. Can I speak to Maria? _____

3. May I speak to Mr. Davis? _____

4. Are your parents home? _____

C *Study and practice.*

Examples.

Questions	Short answers

1. *Are you going* home?   -Yes, *I am.*   -No, *I'm not.*
2. *Is she eating* now?   -Yes, *she is.*   -No, *she's not (she isn't).*
3. *Is Tom working* tonight? -Yes, *he is.*   -No, *he's not (he isn't).*
4. *Is it raining?*   -Yes, *it is.*   -No, *it's not (it isn't).*
5. *Are your children sleeping?* -Yes, *they are.* -No, *they're not (they aren't).*

Write the short answers, then practice with another student.

1. How's your party going?   It's going real good!

2. Is Kathy singing?   Yes, _____

3. Is Martin playing the guitar?   Yes, _____

4. Are the people dancing?   No, _____. They're eating.

5. Is Pete drinking too much?   No, _____

6. Are you watching him?   Yes, _____

7. Are you all having fun?   Yes, _____

D *Complete the conversation, then practice with another student.*

1. Where is your father? — He's in Los Angeles.

2. What's he doing there? — He's working.

3. Where is your mother? — _____ the neighbor's house.

4. What's she doing? — _____

5. Where is your sister? — _____

6. What _____ — _____

7. _____ your brothers? — _____

8. What _____ — _____

9. _____ you doing? — _____ babysitting.

Asking and Giving Directions

Practice this conversation.

Excuse me, which way is the Post Office ?

It's that way.

How far is it?

About 4 blocks.

What street is it on?

On E Street.

Where on E Street ?

Near 8th Avenue.

Thank you.

Change the conversation and practice with another student.

1. the bank
   6 blocks
   on B Street
   near 7th Avenue

2. the bus stop
   3 blocks
   on Broadway
   near 4th Avenue, in front of the bookstore

3. the Chinese restaurant
   2 blocks
   on 5th Avenue
   between E and F, across from the movie theater

4. the drugstore
   5 blocks
   at the corner of 1st and A

5. the park
   1 mile
   on Park Boulevard
   past Washington St.

Downtown

Study the map.

A *Answer the questions.*

1. Where is the post office?   -It's on __E Street__ near __8th Avenue.__

2. Where is the bank?   -It's on _____ near _____.

3. Where is the high school?   -It's on _____ between _____ and _____ .

4. Where is the drugstore?   -It's on the corner of _____ and _____ .

5. Where is the bus stop?   -It's on _____ in front of the _____.

6. What street is the sandwich shop on?   -It's on _____ near _____.

7. What street is the movie theater on?   -It's on _____ across from the _____.

8. What street is the parking lot on?   -It's on _____ between _____ and _____ .

B *Answer the questions.*

1. How far is the post office from the bus stop?   __5 blocks__

2. How far is the bus stop from the post office?   _____

3. How far is the sandwich shop from the bank?   _____

4. How far is the bookstore from the high school?   _____

5. How far is the parking lot from the movie theater?   _____

6. How far is it from the parking lot to the movie theater?   _____

7. How far is it from the bus stop to the high school?   _____

8. How far is it from the post office to the drug store?   _____

Now practice all the questions and answers with another student.

The City

Study the map. Then fill in the blanks.

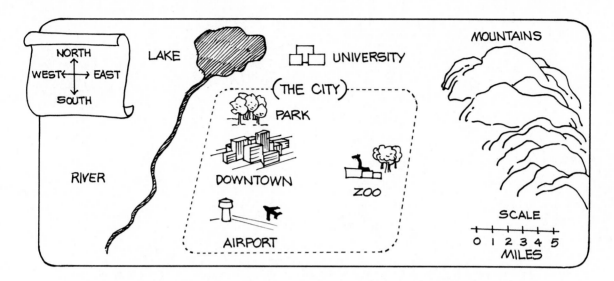

A *Look at the scale on the map and tell how far. Measure with your pencil.*

1. The park is __1__ mile from downtown.

2. The lake is _____ miles from the university.

3. The zoo is _____ miles from downtown.

4. The airport is _____ miles from the river.

5. The park is _____ miles from the zoo.

B *Tell what direction.*

1. The park is __north__ of downtown.

2. The river is _____ of the city.

3. The zoo is _____ of downtown.

4. The park is _____ of the lake.

5. The mountains are _____ of the city.

C *Fill in the blanks.*

1. The airport is __4__ miles __south__ of downtown.

2. The university is _____ miles _____ of downtown.

3. The park is _____ miles _____ of the river.

4. The lake is _____ miles _____ of the university.

5. The river is _____ miles _____ of the mountains.

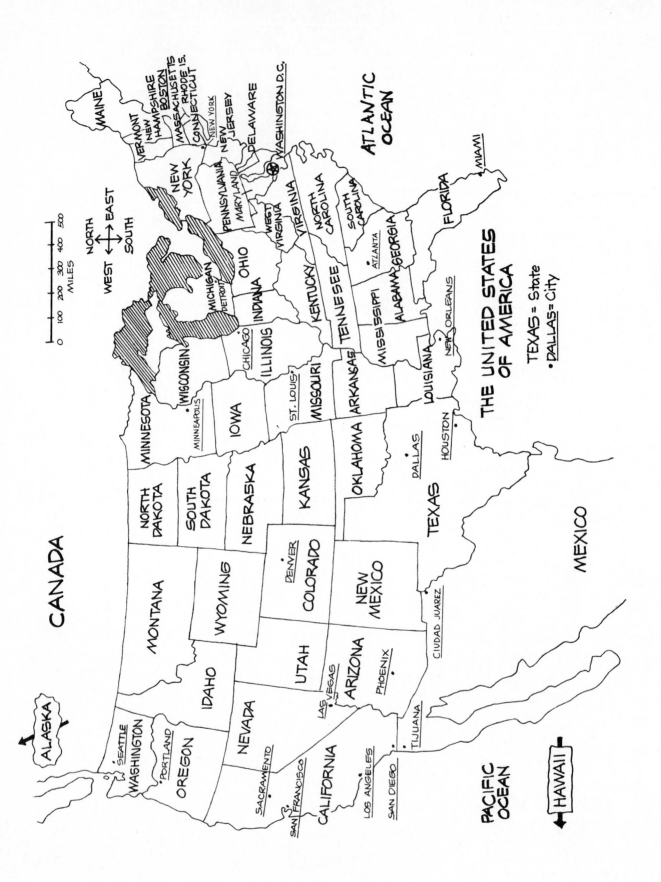

SELF-TEST

A *City or state?*

1. Chicago _____
2. Los Angeles _____
3. Florida _____
4. Texas _____
5. Detroit _____

6. Seattle _____
7. Ohio _____
8. Dallas _____
9. California _____
10. New York _____

B *What part of the country are these states in? (north, south, east, or west)*

1. California _____
2. Texas _____
3. Louisiana _____
4. Virginia _____
5. Pennsylvania _____
6. Wisconsin _____

C *Answer the questions.*

1. What country is north of the United States?

_____

2. What country is south of the United States?

_____

3. What is east of the United States?

_____

4. What is west of the United States?

_____

D *Look at the map and find the distances.*

1. How far is Washington, D.C., from New York City? _____
2. How far is Los Angeles from San Francisco? _____
3. How far is Chicago from San Diego? _____
4. How far is Dallas from Houston? _____
5. How far is it from New York to Los Angeles? _____
6. How far is it from San Francisco to Sacramento? _____
7. How far is it from Denver to St. Louis? _____
8. How far is it from Miami to Seattle? _____

Directions: Walking

Study.

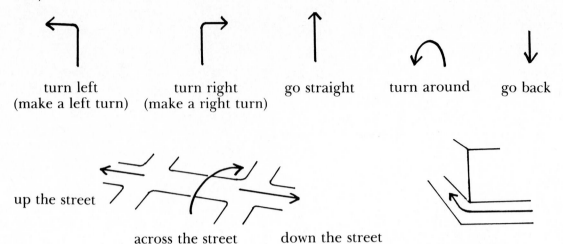

turn left
(make a left turn) turn right
(make a right turn) go straight turn around go back

up the street across the street down the street

around the corner

Practice this conversation.

1. *A:* Excuse me, how do I get to
   the City Office Building ?

   B: Go straight three blocks to E
   Street, then turn right and go
   two blocks. It's on the left.

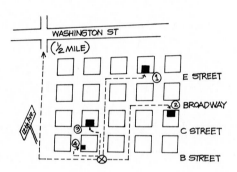

Now change the conversation and practice with another student.

2. *A:* Excuse me, how do I get to the bank?
   B: Turn left at the next corner and go two blocks down to Broadway.
   Turn right and go two blocks. The bank is on the right side of the
   street.

3. *A:* Excuse me, how do I get to the State Employment Office?
   B: Go up here to the next block and turn left. You'll see it across the
   street.

4. *A:* Excuse me, how do I get to the coffee shop?
   B: It's right around the corner.

5. *A:* Excuse me, how do I get to Washington Street?
   B: Go back two blocks and turn right on 12th Avenue. Keep going
   straight on 12th about half a mile. The first big street you come to
   is Washington.

Directions: Driving in the City

Study.

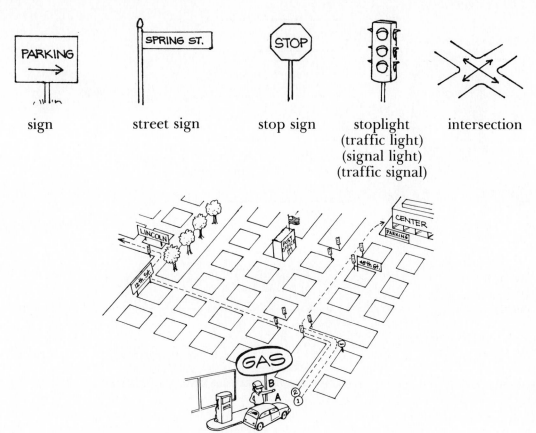

sign   street sign   stop sign   stoplight
                                                        (traffic light)
                                                        (signal light)
                                                        (traffic signal)
                                                                            intersection

Look at the map, and practice these conversations.

1. *A:* Excuse me, how do I get to the shopping center?

   B: Go down here to the stop sign and turn left. Go one block to the stoplight. Turn right and go three blocks to 45th Street. Go one block past the intersection and you'll see the shopping center on the right.

   A: Thanks a lot.

2. *A:* How do I get to Lincoln Avenue?

   B: Go up here to the stop sign and turn left. Go down to the second stoplight—that's 12th Street—and turn right. Then take the first left. That's Lincoln Avenue.

   A: Thank you very much.

Now you give directions.

3. *A:* Excuse me, how do I get to the post office?

   B:

   A: Thank you.

How Do You Go To Work?

Practice this conversation.

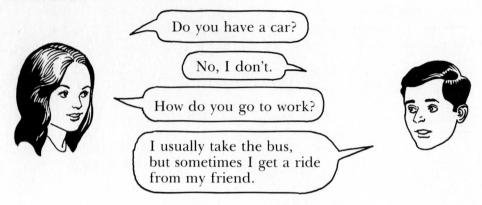

Do you have a car?

No, I don't.

How do you go to work?

I usually take the bus, but sometimes I get a ride from my friend.

Practice.

I take the bus.
I ride the bus.
I go by bus.

I take the train.
I ride the train.
I go by train.

I drive.
My friend drives.
My friend gives me a ride.
I get a ride from my friend.

I fly.
I take a plane.
I go by plane.

I ride my bicycle.
I go by bicycle.

I walk.

Answer these questions. Then practice with another student.

1. Do you have a car?
2. How do you go to school?
3. How do you go to work?
4. How do you go shopping?
5. How do you go downtown?

Orientation Notes: TRANSPORTATION

Read and discuss.

In America you need a car. Almost everybody has a car. Some families have two or three cars. People like to have a car because they can go anywhere at any time. Driving is *convenient*—it's fast and easy.

The streets and highways in America are very good, and it's usually easy to drive around the city or to drive from one city to another. You can also travel by bus, train, or airplane.

Large cities have buses or trains to take people around the city. Some people don't have a car or don't like to drive, and they can take the bus or train.

The money you pay to ride the bus or train is the *fare*. There are different fares for different people; sometimes children, students, and old people *(senior citizens)* pay a low fare. Some cities have a bus *pass* or train pass you can buy every month at a low price.

You pay when you get on the bus. Usually you need *exact change* for the bus, because the driver doesn't have any change. Sometimes you can change from one bus to another bus or to a train and pay only once. You can get a *transfer* from the driver to change buses.

If you need information, ask the driver. He can give you a *schedule* and *route map*.

What bus do I take?
Where can I catch No. 32?
Where do I get off?
What time is the next bus?
What time is the last bus?
What is the Sunday schedule?

Taking the City Bus

Practice this conversation.

> *Man:* What bus goes <u>to the park?</u>
> *Driver:* <u>Number 7.</u>
> *Man:* Where can I catch it? (Where does it stop?)
> *Driver:* <u>Over on 11th and A.</u>
> *Man:* Thanks.

Change the conversation and practice with another student.

1. to Washington Street
   No. 26
   at 5th and E

2. to the hospital
   No. 5B
   over there on the corner

3. downtown
   No. 115
   at 54th and University

4. to Oak Park
   No. 60
   on 12th Avenue

5. to the shopping center
   No. 25 or No. 4
   across the street

6. to the airport
   No. 2
   at 4th and Pine, on the
   north side of the street

■ *action sequence:* ➡
taking the bus

1. Go to the bus stop.
2. Wait for the bus.
3. The bus is coming!
4. Take out your change.
5. The bus stops.
6. The door opens.
7. Get on the bus.
8. Put your money in the box.
9. (Ask the driver for a transfer.)
10. Take a seat.
11. Ride!
12. Pull the cord. (Push the button.)
13. Go to the exit door.
14. The bus stops.
15. The door opens.
16. Get off the bus.

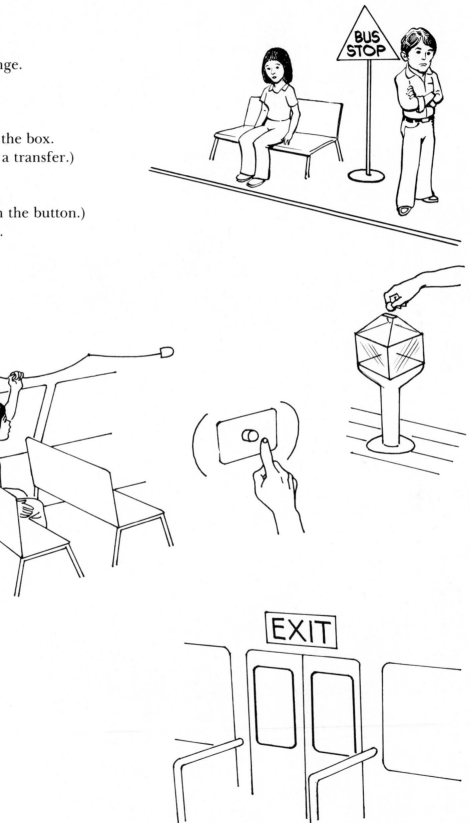

Read and discuss.

If you want to *travel* to another city, and you don't have a car, you can take a bus, a train, or an airplane. Airplanes are usually very expensive. Trains are expensive too. The bus is cheaper, but it takes a long time.

Almost every city has a bus station downtown. Buses leave every day to go to other cities. You can buy a *one-way* ticket (go only) or a *round-trip* ticket (go and come back).

Read and practice.

Tom and his wife are going to visit Tom's uncle in Houston, Texas. They're going to take the bus. They go to the bus company downtown.

Clerk: May I help you?

Tom: Yes, I'd like two tickets to Houston, please.

Clerk: One way or round trip?

Tom: One way; we're going to drive back.

Clerk: That's $85.00 for each ticket, $170.00 total.

Tom: All right. . . . Here.

Clerk: Please put your baggage over here. Thank you. The next bus leaves at 9:20 P.M. from Gate 3.

Tom: Where is Gate 3?

Clerk: At the end of the counter, to the left.

Tom: Thank you.

structure practice

Study.

I'm
she's
they're
etc.
} going to _____

Examples:

1. I'm *going to* walk.
2. She's *going to* drive tomorrow.
3. We're *going to* go to Houston next week.
4. They're *going to* visit Tom's uncle.

A *Complete the sentences.*

1. I usually walk to school, but tomorrow I'm going to take the bus.

2. We usually eat lunch at home, but tomorrow _____
   _____ at a restaurant.

3. She usually goes shopping at the shopping center, but next week
   _____ downtown.

4. The teacher usually gives us homework, but this Friday _____
   _____

5. My friends usually come over to play cards on Saturday, but this week
   _____ on Sunday.

6. I usually leave work at 5:00, but tonight _____
   _____ at 7:00.

B *Complete the conversation.*

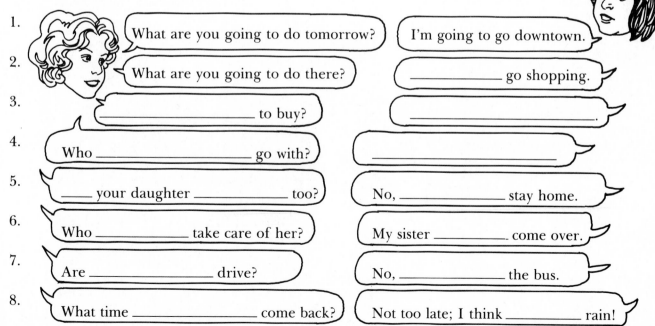

1. What are you going to do tomorrow?   I'm going to go downtown.

2. What are you going to do there?   _____ go shopping.

3. _____ to buy?   _____

4. Who _____ go with?   _____

5. ____ your daughter _____ too?   No, _____ stay home.

6. Who _____ take care of her?   My sister _____ come over.

7. Are _____ drive?   No, _____ the bus.

8. What time _____ come back?   Not too late; I think _____ rain!

Directions and Transportation   **89**

listening and speaking

A *Listen to your teacher pronounce these words. Then listen again and repeat. Then listen to your teacher pronounce the key words below, and write under them the words that have the same sound in the same position. Check the word after you use it (√).*

catch ( )   left ( )   third ( )( )
thank ( )   change ( )   help ( )
push ( )   dish ( )   church ( )( )( )

1	2	3	4	5	6
<u>Ch</u>inese	<u>th</u>eater	mu<u>ch</u>	wa<u>sh</u>	ge<u>t</u>	w<u>or</u>k
_____	_____	_____	_____	_____	_____
_____	_____	_____	_____	_____	_____

Now think, and write one more word for each number.

_____   _____   _____   _____   _____   _____

B *Read the signs and pronounce the street names.*

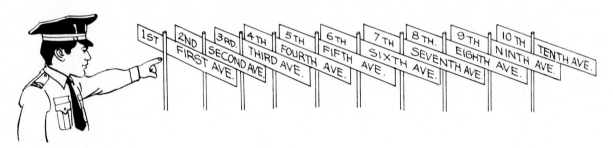

C *Your teacher will pronounce these words. Listen and repeat.*

```
 _   ´  _              ´   _   _          ´   _   _   _        _   _   ´  _        _   _   ´  _  _
con  ve  nient        hos  pi  tal        in  ter  sec  tion    in  for  ma  tion    u  ni  ver  si  ty
                      laun dro mat        ba  by  sit  ting
```

Now pronounce these words and write them above in the correct column.

avenue   employment   bicycle   everybody   Arizona
Washington   Ohio

Health Care

chapter five

COMPETENCIES:
1. Locate and use health care services
2. Make appointments for medical attention
3. Describe physical condition
4. Understand simple diagnosis and instructions
5. Respond to directions
6. Buy prescription medicine and use it appropriately

ORIENTATION:
1. American health care system, including services available, office procedures, clinical procedures, methods of payment
2. Appointments
3. Use of medicine

STRUCTURES:
1. Past tense *be:* affirmative, negative, interrogative, short answers, *wh*-questions
2. Past tense *do* verbs: affirmative, negative, interrogative, short answers, *wh*-questions
3. Imperative and negative imperative
4. Modals: *can, should*
5. Future tense *(will):* affirmative, negative, interrogative, short answers, *wh*-questions

Teacher Notes and Suggestions

Page 94   1. Read through the story while the class follows silently. Ask comprehension questions. Then read again and have the class repeat; then ask further questions.
2. Point out use of past tense in each frame.

Page 95   Relate conversation to picture on preceding page.

Page 96   Introduce, explain, and practice structures orally first. Relate *was* back to page 94.

Page 97   Go back and point out all past forms on page 94. Provide ample practice for these structures and those on the preceding page; they require much more practice than can be given here.

Page 99   1. Relate conversation to page 94. Act out the situation for the class.
2. Mention idea of being on time for appointments.
3. Point out past tense structures.
4. This and all following situations relate to the story on page 94 and may be role-played individually and as a complete story. Follow the suggested procedure (see page *ix*).
5. Point out *will* in the last line as indicating future time.

Page 100   Follow the suggested procedure for presentation and practice.

Page 101   1. Explain the difference between *hurt* and *pain*.
2. Introduce *can/can't*.

Page 102   1. You may present names of parts of the body pointing to yourself first.
2. Vocabulary may be practiced as suggested (see page *ix*).
3. As a test, have students draw a body and label the parts.
4. Point out in 1a that *-s* on the verb *hurts* is used with a singular noun; also, in 1b, the *-s* on the noun *eyes,* etc., denotes a plural noun, and the correspoding verb form has no *-s.* Thus: "My eye hurts" and "My eye*s* hurt."

Page 104   1. "How long have you been sick?" is used as a necessary phrase; present perfect tense should not be taught here.
2. Point out other occurrences of *will.*
3. Follow the suggested procedure for presentation and practice.

Page 105   First demonstrate the actions for the class. Practice as suggested (see page *ix*).

Page 106   Follow the suggested procedure for presentation and practice.

Page 107   1. Review *going to* future; compare with *will* future.
2. Demonstrate each pictured procedure; then drill with the structures.
3. Activity: Form one or two groups of students, calling each a "hospital" or a "clinic." Each student is a doctor or nurse and is assigned to do one of the pictured procedures. Other students are assigned as patients, who go around the hospital to each doctor and ask, "What are you going to do?" Doctors respond according to their task, "I'm going to _____" and act out their task. When all the patients have made the complete circuit, the doctors can change procedures or groups can switch roles.

Page 108   1. Explain use of *should.*
2. Explain about follow-up appointments and use of appointment cards.
3. Follow the suggested procedure for presentation and practice.

Pages 110 to 113   Introduce the structures orally; drill and practice all formations, questions, and answers. Read and practice the examples as a class, then in pairs. Fill in the dialogue exercises for further practice, then practice them orally.

Page 114	Introduce the topic by asking what students do if they're sick: do they know a doctor, or know where a doctor's office is? Do they know where the nearest hospital is? Then ask what they did in their native country when they were sick. Then read the page. Explain in your own words what insurance is and how it works: i.e., many people pay into a company which from those combined resources pays out to cover individual medical costs.
Page 115	1. Follow the suggested procedure for presentation and practice. 2. Key instructions to pictures of medicine bottles.
Page 116	1. Put example medicine bottle on the board. Point out the information, then ask comprehension questions. 2. Point out information on other labels and ask comprehension questions.
Page 117	Introduce the topic by asking if any students take medicine now, if they have medicine at home, if they have gotten medicine from a doctor or bought medicine from a pharmacy. Ask the students where they got medicine in their country. Explain about prescription and nonprescription medicine. Then read the ideas about using medicine.
Page 119	1. Explain and illustrate use of the vocabulary word by word, using translation into students' native languages if necessary and if possible. Often advanced students can explain to others. 2. Use the questions at the bottom for further practice. Point out the use of *ever* in questions and *never* in answers or statements.
Page 120	Introduce the topic by asking if any students have gone to the dentist in America or went in their native country. Explain the vocabulary beforehand, then present and practice the dialogue, following the suggested procedure.

Going to the Doctor

Look at the pictures and read the story.

Last week Ana was sick.

She called Dr. Brown's office at the Health Clinic and made an appointment.

She went to Dr. Brown's office.

She talked to the receptionist.

She filled out a form.

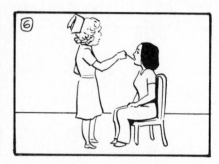

The nurse checked Ana.

Doctor Brown looked at her.

The nurse did some tests.

The doctor gave Ana a prescription for some medicine.

Ana talked to the receptionist before she left.

She went to the drugstore and bought some medicine.

She went home, took her medicine, and went to bed.

Calling the Doctor

Read and practice.

Ana called Dr. Brown's office to make an appointment to see Doctor Brown.

Dr. Brown's office.

Hello. I want to make an appointment to see Doctor Brown.

What's your name?

Ana Lopez.

What's the problem?

I have a headache and a sore throat.

Can you come tomorrow morning at 8:30?

Yes, I can.

Good. See you tomorrow.

Thank you. Goodbye.

Orientation Notes: *MAKING AN APPOINTMENT*

Read and discuss.

If you want to go to a doctor's office to see a doctor, you have to make an appointment. Usually we make an appointment on the telephone. Sometimes it's hard to get the time you want because doctors are usually very busy.

You have to go *on time* for appointments. If you are late, you will have to wait a long time to see the doctor.

If you can't go to an appointment, you have to call to change it or to *cancel* it.

structure practice

Study.

$$\left.\begin{matrix} I \\ he \\ she \\ it \end{matrix}\right\}\quad was(n't) \qquad \left.\begin{matrix} you \\ we \\ they \end{matrix}\right\}\quad were(n't)$$

Examples:

<table>
<tr><td colspan="2">Affirmative</td><td colspan="2">Negative</td></tr>
<tr><td>1.</td><td>I was sick last week.</td><td>6.</td><td>I wasn't sick last week.</td></tr>
<tr><td>2.</td><td>He was a soldier.</td><td>7.</td><td>He wasn't a soldier.</td></tr>
<tr><td>3.</td><td>The movie was good.</td><td>8.</td><td>The movie wasn't good.</td></tr>
<tr><td>4.</td><td>You were late.</td><td>9.</td><td>You weren't late.</td></tr>
<tr><td>5.</td><td>They were in class yesterday.</td><td>10.</td><td>They weren't in class yesterday.</td></tr>
</table>

	Questions	Short answers	
11.	*Were* you sick?	-Yes, I *was*.	-No, I *wasn't*.
12.	*Was* he a soldier?	-Yes, he *was*.	-No, he *wasn't*.
13.	*Was* the movie good?	-Yes, it *was*.	-No, it *wasn't*.
14.	*Was* I late?	-Yes, you *were*.	-No, you *weren't*.
15.	*Were* they in class yesterday?	-Yes, they were.	-No, they *weren't*.
16.	How *was* the movie?		
17.	Where *were* they yesterday?		

Now practice questions 11–17 with another student, using 1 to 10 or short answers as answers.

Complete the conversations.

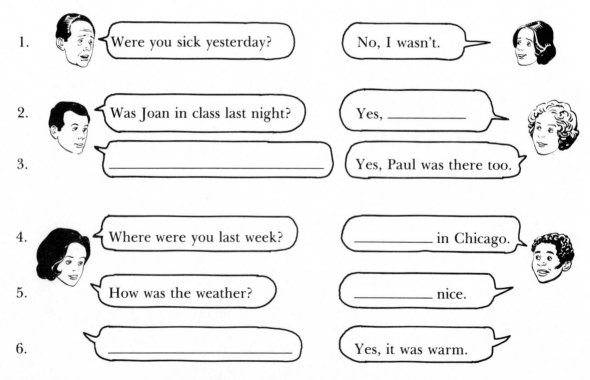

1. Were you sick yesterday? — No, I wasn't.

2. Was Joan in class last night? — Yes, _____

3. _____ — Yes, Paul was there too.

4. Where were you last week? — _____ in Chicago.

5. How was the weather? — _____ nice.

6. _____ — Yes, it was warm.

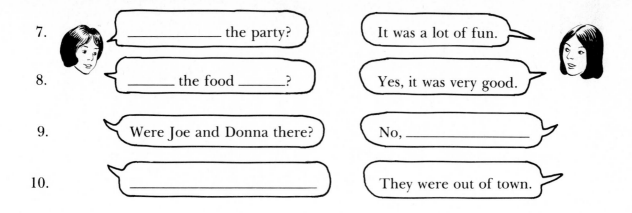

7. _____ the party? — It was a lot of fun.

8. _____ the food _____? — Yes, it was very good.

9. Were Joe and Donna there? — No, _____

10. _____ — They were out of town.

structure practice

Study.

(work)	worked	(live)	lived	(study)	studied	BUT:	
(call)	called	(close)	closed	etc.		(go)	went
	etc.		etc.			(have)	had
						(come)	came
						(take)	took
						(leave)	left
							etc.*

Examples:

Affirmative	Negative
1. I *worked* last night.	6. I *didn't work* last night.
2. Maria *lived* in Texas.	7. Maria *didn't live* in Texas.
3. She *studied* English.	8. She *didn't study* English.
4. We *went* home by bus.	9. We *didn't go* home by bus.
5. They *left* at 8:00.	10. They *didn't leave* at 8:00.

Questions	Short answers	
11. *Did* you *work* last night?	-Yes, I *did*.	-No, I *didn't*.
12. *Did* Maria *live* in Texas?	-Yes, she *did*.	-No, she *didn't*.
13. *Did* she *study* English?	-Yes, she *did*.	-No, she *didn't*.
14. *Did* you *go* home by bus?	-Yes, I *did*.	-No, I *didn't*.
15. *Did* they *leave* at 8:00?	-Yes, they *did*.	-No, they *didn't*.

16. When *did* you *work*?
17. Where *did* Maria *live*?
18. What *did* she *study*?
19. How *did* you *go* home?
20. What time *did* they *leave*?

Now practice questions 11 to 15 with another student, using 1 to 10 or short answers as answers. Then practice questions 16 to 20 with 1 to 5 as answers.

*See Appendix.

Complete the conversations.

1. Did you go to class yesterday?　　Yes, _____

2. _____ about?　　We studied about going to the doctor.

3. Did you understand?　　No, _____ everything.

4. _____ the teacher _____　　Yes, she gave us homework.

5. _____ Sunday?　　I went to Los Angeles.

6. Did you drive?　　No, _____

7. How did you go?　　_____ the bus.

8. How long did you stay there?　　_____ all day.

9. _____ did you go with?　　_____ my sister.

10. _____　　Yes, she liked it a lot.

11. _____ did you eat lunch?　　_____ at a Chinese restaurant.

12. What did you have?　　_____ fried rice.

13. _____ anything?　　Yes, I bought a lot.

14. _____　　We got back around 11:00.

15. Did you have fun?　　Yes, _____ .

Ana Talks to the Receptionist

Read and practice.

Ana got to Dr. Brown's office at 8:15. She talked to the receptionist.

Ana:	Hello, I have an appointment with Dr. Brown at 8:30.
Receptionist:	What's your name?
Ana:	Ana Lopez.
Receptionist:	Did you come here before?
Ana:	No, I didn't.
Receptionist:	Please fill out this form.
Ana:	All right.
Receptionist:	Do you have insurance?
Ana:	Yes.
Receptionist:	Please give me your insurance card.
Ana:	Here.
Receptionist:	Thank you. Please have a seat. The nurse will call you in a few minutes.

The Nurse Sees Ana

Read and practice.

Ana waited. Then a nurse came in and called her name.

Nurse: Ana Lopez?
Ana: Yes?
Nurse: Follow me, please.

She went into the nurse's office. The nurse had a thermometer.

Nurse: What's the problem?
Ana: I have a headache and a sore throat.
Nurse: Sit down here, please, and put this under your tongue.

The nurse took her pulse, then she read the thermometer.

Nurse: You have a low fever. Are you taking any medicine now?
Ana: No, I'm not.

The nurse gave Ana a gown.

Nurse: Go to Room F. Take off your clothes and put on the gown. The doctor will be in to see you.
Ana: Where is Room F?
Nurse: Turn right, then go straight. It's on the left.

What's the Problem?

Study and practice.

1. I have a _____.

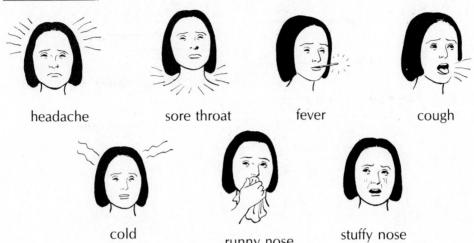

headache   sore throat   fever   cough

cold   runny nose   stuffy nose

2. My _____ hurts.

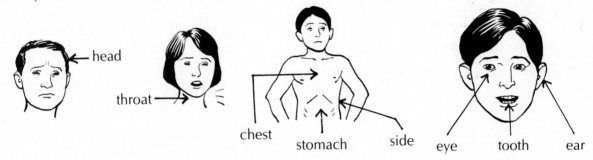

head   throat   chest   stomach   side   eye   tooth   ear

3. I have a pain in my _____.

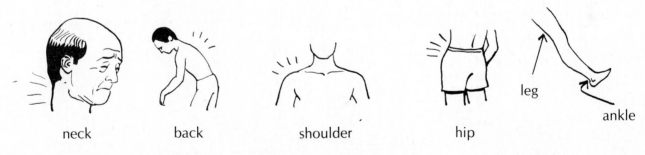

neck   back   shoulder   hip   leg   ankle

4. I can't _____.

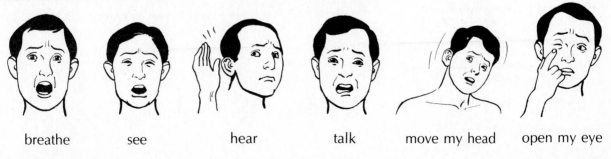

breathe   see   hear   talk   move my head   open my eye

THE BODY

Study these words.

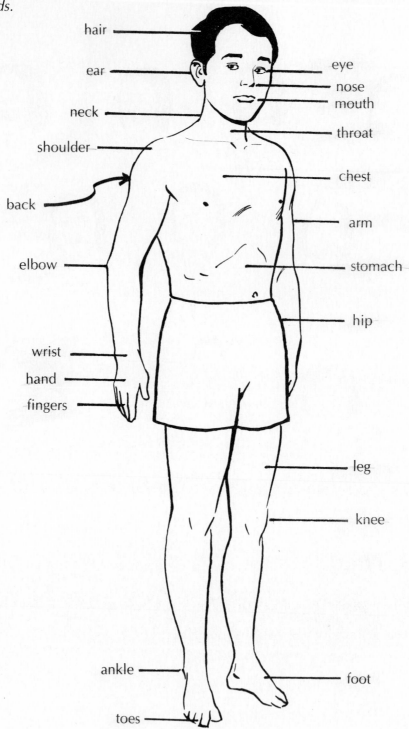

hair
ear
neck
shoulder
back
elbow
wrist
hand
fingers
ankle
toes

eye
nose
mouth
throat
chest
arm
stomach
hip
leg
knee
foot

Practice, with different parts of the body.

1. a. My _____ hurts.

   b. My _____ hurt.

2. I hurt my _____.

SELF-TEST

A *Look back at Ana's story and put the following in order:*

_____ The nurse did some tests.

_____ Ana filled out a form.

__1__ Ana called Doctor Brown's office.

_____ The nurse checked Ana.

_____ The doctor gave her a prescription.

_____ Ana went to Dr. Brown's office.

_____ The doctor looked at her.

B *Answer the questions.*

1. Why did Ana call Dr. Brown's office?

_____

2. What time was her appointment?

_____

3. What time did she get to the office?

_____

4. Was she late?

_____

C

What's the problem?

1. _____

2. _____

3. _____

4. _____

The Doctor Sees Ana

Read and practice.

The doctor came in to see Ana.

Doctor: Hello. Your name is Ana?

Ana: Yes.

Doctor: What's the problem?

Ana: My throat hurts and I have a bad headache. I have a cough and a fever, and I feel very weak.

Doctor: Open your mouth, stick out your tongue, and say "A-a-a-h!"

Let me listen to your chest and your back. Take a deep breath; let it out.

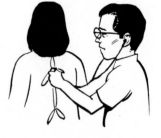

Where does your head hurt?

Ana: Here in front and in back.

Doctor: How long have you been sick?

Ana: About four days.

Doctor: I think you have a flu or virus infection. I'll give you some medicine for your headache and fever, and for your cough. Go back to Room B. The nurse will do some tests.

Ana: Thank you, doctor.

Sit down.
Stand up.
Turn around.
Don't turn around.
Lie down.
Turn over.
Turn on your side.
Move your leg.
Don't move your leg.
Don't move.
Raise your arm.
Raise your left leg.
Sit up.
Breathe in.
Breathe out.
Breathe hard.
Don't breathe.
Take a deep breath and hold it.
Turn your head.
Don't turn your head.
Cough.
Cover your mouth.
Cover your left ear.
Cover your right eye.
Look straight ahead.
Look to the right.
Look to the left.
Don't move your head.
Look up.
Look down.
Look at me.
Don't look at me.
Don't look.
Put your head down.
Put your head back.
Move your head around.
Open your mouth.
Stick out your tongue.

> Look to the left. Don't move your head!

Say "A-a-a-h-h!"
Take off your shirt.
Don't be shy.
Put on a gown.
Don't take off your shoes.
Bend over.
Touch your toes.
Stand up straight.
Touch your shoulders.
Raise your right arm.
Hold up your left arm.
Put your arms down.
Hold out your hand.
Hold out your arm.
Roll up your sleeve.
Make a fist.
Squeeze.
Relax.
Have a seat.

The Nurse Does Some Tests

Read and practice.

Ana went to room B. The nurse talked to her.

Nurse: Miss Lopez, I have to do some tests. Please sit in that chair and roll up your sleeve.

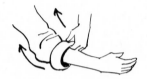

First I'll take some blood.

Now I'll take a throat culture.

Now take this bottle and give me a urine sample.

Ana: Sorry, I don't understand.
Nurse: Go to the bathroom over there, and bring me back the bottle.
Ana: Oh. All right.

When Ana came back, the nurse said:

Nurse: OK, you can put on your clothes now. Put your gown in that basket over there.

What Are You Going to Do?

Study and practice.

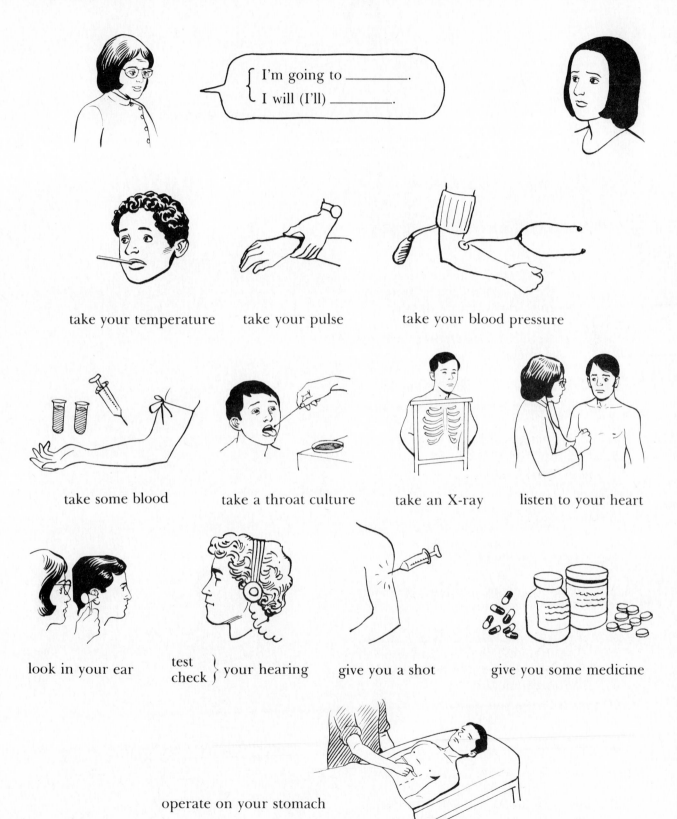

I'm going to _____.
I will (I'll) _____.

take your temperature   take your pulse   take your blood pressure

take some blood   take a throat culture   take an X-ray   listen to your heart

look in your ear   test / check } your hearing   give you a shot   give you some medicine

operate on your stomach

The Nurse Talks to Ana

Read and practice.

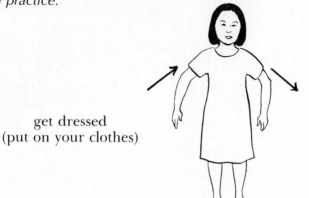

get dressed
(put on your clothes)

get undressed
(take off your clothes)

After Ana got dressed, the nurse talked to her again.

Nurse: Miss Lopez, the doctor says you should rest in bed, stay warm, and drink a lot of water.

Here is a prescription for some medicine.

Ana: Where can I get the medicine?

Nurse: You have to go to a drugstore or pharmacy. There's one on the corner of University Avenue and 30th Street.

Ana: Thank you.

Nurse: Go back out and see the receptionist before you leave. If you still feel bad after three days, call and make an appointment to come in again.

Ana went out to the waiting room and stopped to see the receptionist.

Receptionist: All right, Miss Lopez. You can go now. Take this card and call us if you need to make another appointment.

Ana: Thank you. Goodbye.

SELF-TEST

A *Fill in the blanks.*

1. _____ your mouth

2. _____ your tongue

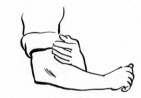

3. _____ your sleeve

4. _____ your arm

5. _____ your clothes

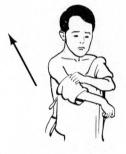

6. _____ a gown

B *What was wrong with Ana? Look back at the story.*

1. <u>She had a bad headache.</u> _____

2. _____

3. _____

4. _____

5. _____

C *What tests did the nurse do?*

1. _____

2. _____

3. _____

D *The doctor said Ana should:*

1. _____

2. _____

3. _____

structure practice

Study.

	Examples:
(I) can _____	I *can* see.
(I) cannot _____ (I can't)	I *can't* see.
Can (you) _____ ?	*Can* you see?

A *Study these examples. Then practice with another student.*

Questions	Answers	Short answers
1. *Can* you see?	-Yes, I *can* see. -No, I *can't* see.	-Yes, I *can*. -No, I *can't*.
2. *Can* she breathe?	-Yes, she *can* breathe. -No, she *can't* breathe.	-Yes, she *can*. -No, she *can't*.
3. When *can* you come?	-I *can* come next Thursday.	
4. What *can* I take for my cough?	-You *can* take this medicine.	
5. Where *can* she buy medicine?	-She *can* buy it at the drugstore.	

B *Complete the conversation, using* **can.** *Then practice with another student.*

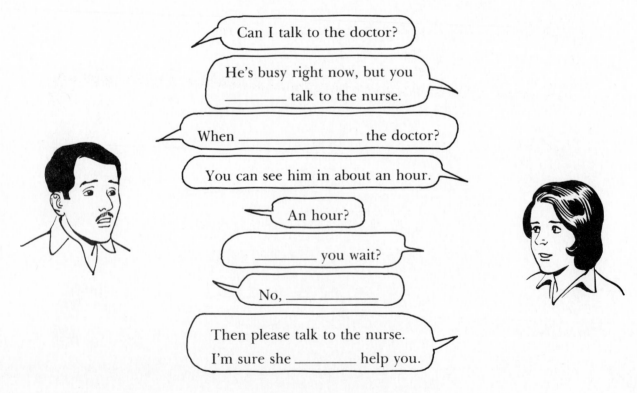

Can I talk to the doctor?

He's busy right now, but you _____ talk to the nurse.

When _____ the doctor?

You can see him in about an hour.

An hour?

_____ you wait?

No, _____

Then please talk to the nurse. I'm sure she _____ help you.

structure practice

Study.

(You) should _____

(You) should not _____ (You shouldn't)

Should (I) _____?

Examples:

You *should* take medicine.

You *shouldn't* take medicine.

Should I take medicine?

A *Study these examples. Then practice with another student.*

Questions	Answers	Short answers
1. My head hurts. *Should* I take my medicine?	-Yes, you *should* take medicine. -No, you *shouldn't* take medicine.	-Yes, you *should*. -No, you *shouldn't*.
2. She doesn't feel well. *Should* she stay in bed?	-Yes, she *should* stay in bed. -No, she *shouldn't* stay in bed.	-Yes, she *should*. -No, she *shouldn't*.
3. What *should* they do?	-They *should* see a doctor.	
4. Where *should* I go?	-You *should* go to the X-ray department.	
5. What *should* I eat?	-You *should* eat more vegetables.	

B *Complete the conversation, using* **should.** *Then practice with another student.*

You have the flu. You should stay home and rest.

_____ I go to work?

No, _____

What _____ I eat?

You _____ eat clear soups, and you _____ drink plenty of liquids. You _____ eat any heavy foods.

All right.

Take this medicine; you _____ feel better in a few days.

When _____ I call you?

Call me on Thursday.

Thank you, doctor.

structure practice

Study.

(I) will _____ (I'll)
(I) will not _____ (I won't)
Will (you) _____?

Examples:
I'll go.
I *won't* go.
Will you go?

Examples:

Affirmative

1. *I'll* see the doctor.
2. *She'll* go back next week.
3. *He'll* stay in the hospital tonight.
4. The doctor *will* give you medicine.
5. *It'll* take a long time.

Negative

6. I *won't* see the doctor.
7. She *won't* go back next week.
8. He *won't* stay in the hospital tonight.
9. The doctor *won't* give you medicine.
10. It *won't* take a long time.

Questions

11. *Will* you see the doctor?
12. *Will* she go back next week?
13. *Will* he stay in the hospital tonight?
14. *Will* the doctor give you medicine?
15. *Will* it take a long time?

16. Who *will* you see?
17. When *will* she go back?
18. Where *will* he stay tonight?
19. What *will* the doctor give you?
20. How long *will* it take?

Short answers

-Yes, I *will.*   -No, I *won't.*
-Yes, she *will.*   -No, she *won't.*
-Yes, he *will.*   -No, he *won't.*
-Yes, he *will.*   -No, he *won't.*
-Yes, it *will.*   -No, it *won't.*

Now practice questions 11 to 15 with another student, using 1 to 10 or short answers as answers. Then practice questions 16 to 20 with 1 to 5 as answers.

Complete the conversation using **will**, **can**, *and* **should**.

Did you know it's Kathy's birthday Saturday?

No, I didn't know. _____ you have a party for her?

Yes, we will. _____ you come?

Sure I can. Where _____ it be?

_____ at Sarah's house.

_____ a lot of people go?

Around fifteen.

What about food? _____ I bring something?

Yes, maybe you should.
Everybody _____ bring something.
_____ you bring some drinks?

Sure. What kind _____ I get?

Just get soft drinks;
no one _____ want beer.
Can you bring your brother's camera?

Sorry, I _____. He's using it.

That's all right. We _____ use mine.

Tell me—how old _____ Kathy be?

I don't know—she _____ tell me!

Now practice with another student.

Orientation Notes: *WHEN YOU'RE SICK*

Read and discuss.

What should you do when you're sick?

1. If you're a little sick, take it easy. Rest after work.
2. If you're very sick, don't go to work or to school. Go see a doctor.
3. If you have an emergency, go to the hospital fast, or call an ambulance (paramedics) or the operator.

Where should you go when you're sick?

1. Go to a doctor. Some doctors have an office, and some are in clinics. If you don't know a doctor, ask your friends.
2. Go to the *Public Health Service*. They can help you with some things.
3. In an emergency, go to the hospital near your house. Go to the Emergency Room.

In America *health care* is not free. You have to pay. How can you pay?

1. Pay the doctor yourself. Sometimes you have to pay before you leave the office; sometimes the doctor will send you a *bill.*
2. Get *insurance.* The insurance company will pay for you. Usually you can get health insurance from your job. Sometimes your company will pay for your insurance; sometimes you have to pay.
3. Use Medicaid (Medical) or Medicare. Sometimes the government can help poor people or old people pay their medical bills.

Health care is expensive!

At the Drugstore

Read and practice.

Ana went to the drugstore at the corner of University and 30th. She talked to a clerk.

Ana:	Excuse me. Where can I buy medicine?
Clerk:	Do you have a prescription?
Ana:	Yes.
Clerk:	At that counter over there, under the PRESCRIPTIONS sign.
Ana:	Thank you.

She went to the prescription counter and talked to the pharmacist.

Ana:	Hello. Can you fill this prescription, please?
Pharmacist:	Yes. It'll take about ten minutes.

Later he gave Ana her medicine.

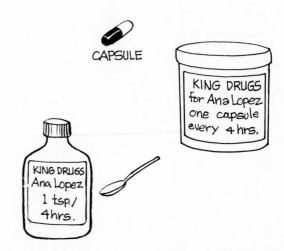

Pharmacist:	This is for your fever and headache. Take one capsule every four hours, before meals. There are 25 capsules here. If you need more, come back.
	This is for your cough. Take one teaspoon every four hours.
	That's $6.78.
Ana:	Here.
Pharmacist:	Thank you.

Health Care   **115**

Medicine and Directions

Study the label.

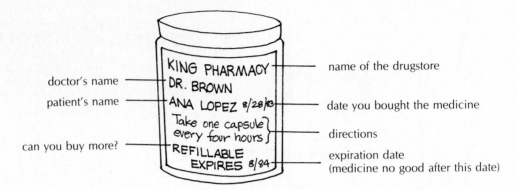

Read the directions on the labels and answer the questions.

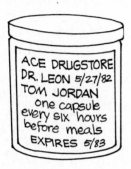

a. What's the doctor's name?
b. When did Mr. Jordan buy the medicine?
c. What are the directions?

a. What are the directions?
b. What is the medicine for?
c. Can Ms. Adamson buy more?

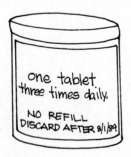

a. What are the directions?
b. Can I buy more?
c. When should I throw it away?

a. How much should you take?
b. My daughter is 9 years old. How much should I give her?
c. Can I give this medicine to my baby?

Orientation Notes: *MEDICINE*

Read and discuss.

You can buy medicine at the drugstore or pharmacy. For some medicine you need a prescription from your doctor. For other medicine (aspirin, sometimes cough medicine) you don't need a prescription.

Using medicine

1. Read the directions before you take medicine.
2. Don't take medicine every time you have a little headache. Only take medicine if you really need it.
3. When you take medicine, don't stop after one or two pills if you're still sick. Take enough medicine, but don't take too much.
4. If you finish your medicine and you need more, the pharmacy can sometimes refill your prescription. Sometimes for strong medicine you can't get a refill, and you have to go back to your doctor and get a new prescription.
5. Your medicine is only for you. Don't give it to somebody else.
6. Don't give adult medicine to a child. Ask your doctor or the pharmacist for the right medicine.
7. Don't take medicine and drink liquor together.
8. Some medicine can make you sleepy; don't drive a car.
9. Sometimes medicine makes you sick, because you are *allergic* to it. Stop taking it, and tell the doctor.
10. Don't use old medicine. If you get sick, go see the doctor again.
11. Throw old medicine away after a long time (after it *expires*). If you have children at home, don't put the medicine in the wastebasket. Pour it down the toilet.
12. Put medicine away in a high cabinet.

SELF-TEST

A *What is it?*

_____   _____   _____   _____

B *Read the directions on the medicine bottle and answer the questions.*

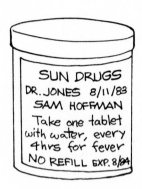

1. What's the doctor's name? _____
2. What's the patient's name? _____
3. When did he buy the medicine? _____
4. What's the name of the drugstore? _____
5. What are the directions? _____
6. Can he buy more of this medicine? _____
7. When should he throw the medicine away? _____

C *Good or bad?*

_____ 1. I give my medicine to my friend.

_____ 2. I throw old medicine away.

_____ 3. I put medicine away in a high cabinet.

_____ 4. I took two pills and I'm still sick. I think I'll stop taking this medicine.

_____ 5. I drink whiskey when I'm taking medicine.

_____ 6. I feel a little headache. I think I'll take some medicine.

_____ 7. Aspirin is not strong. I'll take five or six.

_____ 8. I read the directions on the label before I take medicine.

HEALTH VOCABULARY

Study these words.

1. physician (doctor)
2. patient (sick person)
3. medical history
4. physical examination
5. check-up
6. laboratory
7. disease
8. cancer
9. lungs
10. tuberculosis
11. TB skin test
12. operate, operation (surgery)
13. stitches
14. influenza (flu)
15. injection (shot)
16. immunization, inoculation (shot against disease)
17. blind
18. deaf
19. hearing aid
20. infection
21. antiseptic
22. bandage
23. muscle
24. bone
25. cast
26. crutches
27. urine
28. stool
29. diarrhea
30. constipation
31. allergy, allergic
32. rash
33. itch
34. scratch
35. swell, swelled, swollen
36. break, broke, broken
37. sprain, sprained
38. burn, burned
39. heal, healed
40. bleed, bled
41. sweat (perspire)
42. sneeze
43. choke
44. vomit (throw up)
45. nausea, nauseous
46. dizzy
47. unconscious
48. ill (sick)
49. condition
50. serious
51. normal
52. pregnant
53. labor pains (in labor)
54. give birth
55. birth control
56. contraceptive
57. family planning
58. specialist
59. pediatrician (doctor for children)
60. obstetrician (doctor for giving birth)
61. gynecologist (doctor for women)
62. optometrist (eye doctor)

Answer the questions.

1. Did you ever have a physical examination in the United States?
2. Did you ever have a TB skin test?
3. Did you ever have surgery?
4. Do you have antiseptic at home?
5. Did you ever break a bone?
6. Are you allergic to anything?
7. Do you know about birth control?
8. Do you have a family doctor?

At the Dentist's Office

Read and practice.

Ana took her niece to the dentist's office. Ana talked to the receptionist.

Receptionist:	May I help you?
Ana:	We want to see the dentist. I have an appointment for 2:30.
Receptionist:	Are you a new patient?
Ana:	Yes.
Receptionist:	Please fill out this form and take a seat.

A few minutes later the dentist's assistant came in and talked to Ana.

Assistant:	Hello, Miss Lopez. What can we do for you today?
Ana:	Please clean and check my teeth, and look at my niece's teeth. She has a toothache.
Assistant:	Come in and we'll talk to Dr. Smith.
Dr. Smith:	Hello, Miss Lopez. You said your niece has a toothache? Let me see. Which tooth hurts?
Ana:	This one on top in back.
Dr. Smith:	All right, I'll take a look at it.
Ana:	Please fill the tooth—don't pull it out.
Dr. Smith:	Don't worry. It doesn't look too bad, but I want to take an X-ray first. If she has a cavity, I'll fill it. Before I drill, I'll give her a shot of Novocain. It won't hurt.

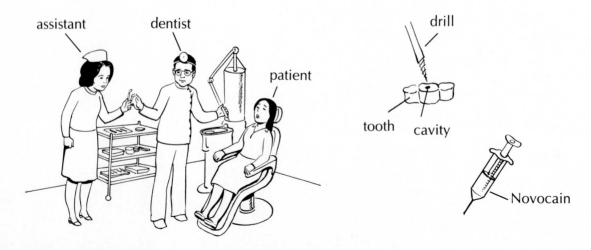

listening and speaking

A *Listen to your teacher pronounce these words. Then listen again and repeat. Then listen to your teacher pronounce the key words below, and write under them the words that have the same sound in the same position. Check the word after you use it (✓).*

hip ( )   deep ( )   mouth ( )   good ( )
door ( )   shy ( )   half ( )   warm ( )
cough ( )   gown ( )( )   sure ( )

1	2	3	4	5	6
<u>g</u>ive	<u>sh</u>oe	to<u>p</u>	o<u>ff</u>	<u>now</u>	m<u>ore</u>

_____ _____ _____ _____ _____ _____

_____ _____ _____ _____ _____ _____

Now think, and write one more word for each number.

_____ _____ _____ _____ _____ _____

B *Listen to the pronunciation of the final sounds. Then read each column and pronounce carefully.*

I		II		III
tal<u>ked</u>	fini<u>shed</u>	st<u>ayed</u>	clean<u>ed</u>	want<u>ed</u>
wor<u>ked</u>	wat<u>ched</u>	stud<u>ied</u>	clo<u>sed</u>	need<u>ed</u>
stop<u>ped</u>	coug<u>hed</u>	cal<u>led</u>	chang<u>ed</u>	wait<u>ed</u>
dres<u>sed</u>		li<u>ved</u>	answ<u>ered</u>	rest<u>ed</u>

C *Your teacher will pronounce these words. Listen and repeat.*

‒ ´
ex pire

‒ ´ ‒   ´ ‒ ‒   ‒ ´ ‒ ‒
ap point ment yes ter day re cep tio nist
in su rance   me di cine
as sis tant   phar ma cy

Now pronounce these words and write them above in the correct column.

operate prescription infection Saturday thermometer directions _

Appendix

irregular verbs

Base Form	Past	Past Participle	Base Form	Past	Past Participle
be	was	been	know	knew	known
break	broke	broken	leave	left	left
bring	brought	brought	lose	lost	lost
buy	bought	bought	make	made	made
catch	caught	caught	meet	met	met
come	came	come	put	put	put
cost	cost	cost	read	read	read
cut	cut	cut	ride	rode	ridden
do	did	done	ring	rang	rung
drink	drank	drunk	run	ran	run
drive	drove	driven	say	said	said
eat	ate	eaten	see	saw	seen
fall	fell	fallen	sell	sold	sold
feel	felt	felt	send	sent	sent
fight	fought	fought	sing	sang	sung
find	found	found	sit	sat	sat
fit	fit	fit	sleep	slept	slept
fly	flew	flown	speak	spoke	spoken
forget	forgot	forgotten	spend	spent	spent
freeze	froze	frozen	steal	stole	stolen
get	got	gotten	take	took	taken
give	gave	given	teach	taught	taught
go	went	gone	tell	told	told
have	had	had	think	thought	thought
hear	heard	heard	understand	understood	understood
hit	hit	hit	wake	woke	woken
hurt	hurt	hurt	win	won	won
keep	kept	kept	write	wrote	written